"Making people cry is easy. Making people laugh is hard. Teaching people how to make other people laugh is even harder. Keith Giglio does it in this book in a straightforward and humorous way!"
— Alan R. Cohen & Alan Freedland, Writers/Producers of *Due Date, King of the Hill, American Dad*

"It'll light a fire under your ass — and not in a teen comedy kind of way. Inspirational, practical, and a great read unto itself. Keith's book will help you write not only a great comedy screenplay but also any genre of screenplay."
— Michael Davis, Writer/Director of *Shoot 'Em Up, Eight Days a Week*

"This book is not only about Blockbuster Comedy... it reads like one! Sharp, funny, and focused on the practical and commercial, Keith Giglio has crafted the essential handbook for writing modern film comedy — for anyone ambitious and twisted enough to try!"
— Tom Brady, Writer/Director of *The Animal, The Hot Chick, Bucky Larson: Born To Be A Star*

"Keith Giglio's *Writing the Comedy Blockbuster* is a must-read for all comedy writers — working or not working — student or pro. It is entertaining, inspirational, and packed full of valuable information."
— Tom Martin, Two-time Emmy Award winner for Fox TV's *The Simpsons*

"Finally, a funny book about being funny from someone who is and has actually made a living at it. This is a wonderfully entertaining screenwriting class school... in 200 pages. I hope both screenwriters and producers decide to enroll."
— Lisa Bruce, Producer, *No Strings Attached*

"Keith Giglio has crafted the essential handbook for writing the comedy screenplay. Teaching that a strong storyline is as important as a clever punchline, Keith guides the reader step by step through the process of turning a clever idea into a funny script. Insightful, educational, and hilarious, this is the how-to book that all aspiring comedy writers needs next to their laptop."
— Carr D'Angelo, Producer, *The Animal, The Hot Chick*

"Giglio's tone is light in this funny, easy read. Highly recommended for screenwriters interested in writing comedies."
— *Library Journal*

"Breezy, accessible, and — above all — useful. Keith Giglio's book won't turn you into a better lover (sorry, Mom), but it WILL help you become a better screenwriter."
— David Breckman, Writer/Producer, *Monk, Saturday Night Live*

"Keith Giglio is an amazing writer and an even more amazing teacher. He's got tons of experience, wisdom, and knowledge, and the very rare ability to convey all of it in a clear, easy-to-follow, and entertaining way. Keith is the real deal!"
— Steve Mazur, Co-Writer, *Liar, Liar*

"Keith breaks down the comedy screenplay from concept to completion and does so with a lot of laughs. It's a great 'behind the scenes' tour of the Hollywood writer's process, full of good advice for anyone trying to figure out the business of comedy."
— Michael Bostick, Producer, *Bruce Almighty*

"What Keith has done is nothing less than a comedy version of *The Hero's Journey*, providing writers not only a sequence-by-sequence roadmap for the specific genre, but also a slew of tips, principles, and exercises to create their comedy blockbuster. Think Joseph Campbell meets Judd Apatow."
— Scott Myers, Writer, *K-9*, host of GoIntoTheStory.com

"*Writing the Comedy Blockbuster: The Inappropriate Goal* is not your ordinary, garden variety tome on screenwriting — it's probably one of the most entertaining and informative books on the subject of scripting a comedy! Giglio gives writers valuable in-the-trenches advice partnered with practical, insightful exercises. This read is guaranteed to help you focus on your comedy project as well as tickle your funny bone!"
— Kathie Fong Yoneda, consultant, workshop leader, and author of *The Script-Selling Game: A Hollywood Insider's Look At Getting Your Script Sold and Produced* (2nd edition)

"Keith Giglio has opened my eyes and shut my mouth! I've been writing comedy for 25 years, and have never heard of 'the inappropriate goal.' I have to tell you, it was an eye opener. Knowledge of that, and how to use it to make your comedies really funny, is definitely going to help me in my feature career as well as in my sitcom classes at Loyola Marymount University. If you want to write a comedy, BUY THIS BOOK!"
— Paul Chitlik, Author of *Rewrite: A Step-By-Step Guide to Strengthen Structure, Characters, and Drama in Your Screenplay*

WRITING THE COMEDY BLOCKBUSTER

THE INAPPROPRIATE GOAL

KEITH GIGLIO

MICHAEL WIESE PRODUCTIONS

Published by Michael Wiese Productions
12400 Ventura Blvd. #1111
Studio City, CA 91604
(818) 379-8799, (818) 986-3408 (FAX)
mw@mwp.com
www.mwp.com

Cover design by MWP
Interior design by William Morosi
Copyedited by Annalisa Zox-Weaver
Printed by McNaughton & Gunn

Manufactured in the United States of America

Library of Congress Cataloging-in-Publication Data

Giglio, Keith, 1963-
 Writing the comedy blockbuster : the inappropriate goal / Keith Giglio.
     p. cm.
 ISBN 978-1-61593-085-2
 1. Comedy films--Authorship. I. Title.
 PN1996.G42 2012
 808.2'523--dc23

                              2011039251

Printed on Recycled Stock

CONTENTS

PART ONE: HOW TO USE THIS BOOK

CHAPTER ONE
HOW TO BUST A GUT

CHAPTER TWO
THE COMEDIC IDEA

PART TWO: PLOT VS. CHARACTER: WHO WILL WIN?

Part Three: The Comedic Roadmap — The Eight Comic Sequences

Chapter Five
Comic Sequence (A)

Chapter Six
Comic Sequence (B)

CHAPTER SEVEN
ACT TWO!
A.K.A. WHERE SCRIPTS GO TO DIE
COMIC SEQUENCE (C)

CHAPTER EIGHT
COMIC SEQUENCE (D)

CHAPTER NINE
COMIC SEQUENCE (E)

CHAPTER TEN
COMIC SEQUENCE (F)

CHAPTER ELEVEN
ACT THREE

COMIC SEQUENCE (G)

CHAPTER TWELVE
COMIC SEQUENCE (H)

CHAPTER THIRTEEN
WRITING THE SCREENPLAY

DEDICATION AND THANK YOUS

Thanks to the Breckmans — to Dave, for friendship and many years of laughter and joy away from Staten Island; and to Andy — for showing me the yellow brick road and for pointing me in the direction of Oz.

Thanks to Dr. Linda Venis and everyone else (then and now) at UCLA Extension for giving me the opportunity to develop the class that became this book.

Thanks to my family (Mom, Dad, Aunt Ella, and my brother and sister, inlaws, outlaws, and all the rest) for putting up with my foolishness.

And special thanks to my Giglio Girls — my daughters, Sabrina and Ava, for laughing at my good jokes, not laughing at the bad ones, and for having such great senses of humor — an amazing feat considering one quarter of your ancestry. I fully expect a "Thank You" note from the two of you for earning a mention in the dedication.

To Juliet, for laughing with me, and for making me laugh and making me smile even when you're yelling at me for something I stupidly said, did, or was thinking of doing. I'm very happy you married this fool.

INTRODUCTION

BY ANDY BRECKMAN

Andy Breckman is a television and film writer and a radio personality. He is the co-creator and executive producer of the Emmy Award-winning television series Monk on the USA Network, and is co-host of WFMU radio's long-running conceptual comedy program Seven Second Delay. He has written screenplays for a number of comedy films including Sgt. Bilko and Rat Race and is frequently hired as a "script doctor" to inject humorous content into scripts written by other screenwriters. He has worked on Saturday Night Live and Late Night with David Letterman.

Let me tell you about my first day in Hollywood.

I had flown to Los Angeles to pitch some movie ideas. I had worked on some TV shows back in New York, but this trip was my first time trying to sell to a major studio. I pulled up to the main gate at Universal Studios. The guard handed me my drive-on pass, and waved me through. My movie geek heart was pounding! I'd been watching — absorbing — movies since I was a kid. All I ever wanted to do was make movies.

Write movies.

That was the dream.

There was a truck in front of me. It stopped. Some workers started loading movie scripts onto the back. They must have been cleaning out a warehouse or something. There were thousands — *tens* of thousands — of scripts piled up in cardboard cartons. I could see their titles — in bright magic markers — handwritten on the spines. Some — I suppose — were movies that had been produced. But most were scripts that had never been made, and never would be made. A truckload of broken dreams.

My heart sank. I felt humbled and intimidated. I suddenly saw what I was up against. In one horrific moment, I understood the odds against me. Each of those scripts had been written by professional screenwriters, right? How could I possibly compete with all of them? Why should I even try?

I pulled over. I was shaking. I wanted to go home.

Since you're reading this, I assume that you have the same dream. Here's my guarantee: You will soon be tested. It will feel like the whole town — the whole industry — is conspiring, in a nutty Oliver Stone sort of way, to break your virgin heart. To discourage you. To send you home. You're going to feel like the guy in that Gladys Knight & the Pips song, "Midnight Train To Georgia." I tear up every time I hear it. "L.A. proved too much for the man..."

Here's my advice: DO NOT GET ON THAT MIDNIGHT TRAIN. If Gladys Knight calls, hang up! Avoid the Pips altogether. Persevere. Wait tables. Drive limos. Take improv classes. Work for free on the set of your roommate's Godawful indie film.

Don't give up. Keep your eyes open. Be prepared to be lucky.

And learn your craft. That's where this book comes in.

As Professor Giglio says... sorry, it feels weird calling him "Professor" — I've known him since he was a kid.

As Mr. Giglio says... no, that doesn't feel right either.

As *Keith* says... this book won't write your script for you. Only you can provide the Divine Spark. Think of this text as an instruction booklet — the kind you get in the carton with your 500-piece Ikea computer desk. It will help you assemble — and arrange and polish — the pieces of your screenplay. What to do first... basic structure... finding a theme.... what pieces go where... molding a comedic character... building conflict!

Making it all fit and work together.

I was lucky. I *couldn't* quit. I was blessed with a complete lack of any other marketable skills. So I stuck it out, and taught myself — by trial and very painful error — how to tell and sell a story. I wish I had this wonderful book back then; it would've saved me a lot of time and heartache. The truth is, I'm kind of pissed off at Keith for not writing it twenty-five years ago.

Here's my hope: that you apply the lessons you learn in these pages and write a brilliantly funny, successful movie, then another, then form a studio-financed production company to oversee other writers and other projects, then remember how helpful and witty this introduction was, then hire me.

— Andy Breckman

FOREPLAY

OR HOW TINA FEY

CAN KICK BRUCE WILLIS' ASS

C omedy is not just the funny bone of the film business. It can also be the backbone. For a writer looking to break into this crazy business, comedy is the shortest road to the land of Oz. Sure, it's a road lined with banana peels — but it's still the shortest road.

Let's imagine another sunny day in Los Angeles. Actors are working out. Actresses are jogging on the beach. Directors are taking meetings.

And writers are waiting.

And worrying.

Because that's what they do. Sometimes even more than writing. Because their scripts are out there, flying around the web, yelling, "Look at me! Look at me!"

A producer — let's call him Mr. Flip-Flops — is at his desk. He's got his latte at the perfect temp. He's just hit the gym. He opens his computer and sees some scripts that have been emailed to him from agents or managers or his development team.

He clicks the PDF file. It's a GREAT BIG ORIGINAL SCIENCE FICTION MOVIE. It's epic. Amazing. Wow. I love this, he thinks, BUT the production is going to cost the studio $200 million, and it's not based on any comic book or TV show or book. There is no preawareness. It's not transmedia. There is no way the studio is going to buy this.

So he snacks on some seaweed. (Yes, that's what they're eating these days. Seaweed).

The producer reads the next script. Let's call it AWESOME URBAN CRIME DRAMA. It's juicy. Sexy. The producer thinks — it's awesome! If we get Marty and Leo or Russell or Denzel it might work. But those guys are booked for the next year. (The producer needs a movie he can make now. The balloon payment on the mortgage is due. His kids are in private school). "I need money!" he thinks.

Now, the latte is cold. The seaweed is making his stomach hurt. His ex-wife is texting him, reminding him of what an ass he can be. He is going to give up for the day. Heck, Mr. Flip-Flops has done a lot of reading today. His head is hurting.

But the next script is shorter. 100 pages. There's a lot of white on the page. It's dialogue driven. The title makes him laugh. Let's call that script: FUNNY IS MONEY. Mr. Flip-Flops cracks open the first page — and laughs. He didn't want to laugh. He was not in a good mood when he started reading a third script in the same morning. But he laughed.

He turns the page.

And laughs again. The script is funny. And it takes place in a small town. One location. Now, he can't stop laughing. And he thinks, if I laughed, someone else will laugh.

The producer then puts on his producer hat and thinks, "I can make this cheap."

Mr. Flip-Flops realizes this comedy script is high concept/low budget. Instead of paying for huge stars, he can find the next big star. He can't afford Steve Carell but he can afford the next Steve Carell. Television is like the minor leagues for comedy stars. Always has been, always will be.

Suddenly that script is taking on a life of its own.

He calls the agent. I loved it.

The agent now calls the other producer who has the script. He tells them Mr. Flip-Flops is interested. Suddenly Miss Addicted to Diet Soda is reading the script and wants to take it to her studio. Mr. Pony-Tail calls in. The script is gaining buzz. Everyone wants to read FUNNY IS MONEY.

The writer is at home. Pacing. Checking emails. Checking his phone.

The phone rings. It's his agent. "People like the script. We're going to the studios."

The writer now can't sleep. It's a bidding war. Different studios are vying to option the script. They want to meet the writer, because...

The writer sells the script.

He calls his Mom and says, "Remember all those dick jokes I used to tell in school? Well, they just made me half a million dollars!"

Ahh, I love this town!

In today's climate of Hollywood (and when I say "Hollywood," I refer to anyone in any part of Los Angeles and neighboring counties who is looking to make a studio-based, mainstream movie) — where corporate-owned studios look for the tent-pole franchise, friendly preawareness, transmedia branded properties like *Spiderman* or *Harry Potter* — it's difficult to sell original material, but it's less difficult to sell an original comedy.

Why is that?

Well, one reason: they tend to be cheaper to make; anywhere from $30-$50 million, as opposed to $150 million and up. *Date Night*'s budget is estimated to be $55 million. Not a low-budget movie, but cheap compared to the $80 million spent on *The Surrogates*. *The Surrogates* made $38 million domestically. *Date Night* has made $98 million domestically.

Tina Fey kicks Bruce Willis' box office ass.

Sweet!

But aside from the budget issues and, as writers, you shouldn't concern yourself too much with the budgetary issues — the simple fact is that if you write something funny on the page, people will laugh.

Laughter is indeed the best medicine for your ailing career.

Chances are you've picked up this book because you like a certain amount of "yucks" in your life; or, you've seen movies like *The Hangover*, *There's Something about Mary*, and *Date Night* and thought — I could write one of those!

Then let's do just that. Because there is not enough laughter in the world.

This book has come out of years of writing comedies for studios and television; of working and living the Hollywood dream — and of surviving the Hollywood nightmare. I have been hired and fired, spent time in the trenches and in the classroom. When teaching students, I notice certain questions crop up time and time again regarding comedy.

"What makes a great comedy screenplay?"

This book is my answer to that question. It's from experience and time spent reading, writing, and watching.

And also from a year of being soft.

No, I am not talking about any personal erectile problems. I am talking about the worst thing a writer can be labeled out here in Hollywood.

Soft.

If you're a comedy writer and you're soft, it's the kiss of death. When my wife and I were breaking in to the business, we did what all writers should do to break into this business. We slept around. No, not true. We're not actors, we're writers. So we wrote... and wrote.

In truth, the first comedy we wrote together secured us an agent. The second comedy, we sold. The third one was passed over by everyone in town, and studio executives began to whisper to our agents — they're soft.

They don't write edgy.

They can't write hard jokes.

They're sweet.

When writing a comedy blockbuster, you want people falling out of their chairs, not falling asleep in their chairs. You want a HA, not an AHHH. An AHHH means sweet, cute.

We were sweet and cute... and not getting work.

So we set out to write an R-Rated comedy that would sell (it never did) and get us work (it did, lots of it).

As our bank account dwindled and our spirits deflated, we wrote a comedy that would be called *Beer Boy*. It was about a brewmaster, a "Henry Higgins of beer" who is jilted at the altar and loses his ability to taste beer. When he learns his ex-fiancee is getting married, he decides to ruin her wedding the way she ruined his life. In the end, he learns that revenge is bad and gets his taste back.

It was the antiromantic comedy.

Broad. Funny... and our agent hated it.

Hated it.

He would not send it out.

"This script will hurt you," he told us over dinner. It reminded me of the scene in *Jerry Maguire* where Jerry is fired in a public place so he doesn't lose it.

We had spent months writing this script. Now what?

Our manager liked it. So he slipped it… to a couple of other agencies. Pretty big agencies.

They read it. We had offers the next day to sign with them. We went with ICM after Juliet asked our agent: "What happens if the script goes out and doesn't sell?"

"I'll get you work off this script," the agent replied.

The script went out — with beer. Yes, we sent it out with beer.

And everyone loved it. And it didn't sell.

We thought it was going to. But it didn't happen. But a funny thing did happen — our careers. The phone began to ring. People felt we could write comedic characters and jokes.

And we were no longer soft. We had a script that had an erection that lasted longer than four hours.

And we got work. Lots of it.

I've learned that even if a script doesn't sell, the writer can. Let's write the best script possible and let the chips fall where they may. I really do believe that the cream rises to the top in Hollywood and that a good script never goes unnoticed.

They are few and far between.

I will guide you from knowing what a comedy blockbuster is to knowing how to write one. We will progress step by step, building from logline, to character, to theme, to the comedic chapters that are going to become your set-pieces, to story.

The hard part of writing is breaking the story. Or figuring out what to write.

Writing a feature film script is a marathon, not a sprint; and the key to completing it lies in training and preparation. If you've had the experience of leaping into the creative process — fingers dancing across the keyboard, pages coming fast, visions of the sequel — only to peter out by page thirty or forty, or if you are a first-time screenwriter, this book is for you. It shows you how to map out your comedy so that you can see plot holes pages away and, at the same time, instill it with your passion and personal vision. When you're finished reading the book and writing your outline — the script will flow.

You don't begin writing the screenplay until you know what the screenplay is going to be about. We break the story first. Characters. Plots. Pay-offs.

It won't be easy. Screenwriting never is. Staring at a blank page all day long is a hard way to make an easy living.

I think this book will make your writing life a little easier and your screenplay a lot funnier.

PART ONE

HOW TO
USE THIS BOOK

I admit that the idea of writing a chapter on how to use this book seems odd. Especially to me, and I am writing it.

When my wonderful editor proposed this idea, I thought: Don't you just read the book, and do what the book says to do? But then I thought about you — in the bookstore, on your commute, in the bathroom (hold on — backspace, delete that image) — and your comedy blockbuster dreams.

Did you ever order something that came in a box? With lots of screws? And parts? And press-wood? With instructions on how to put it together? Well, think of this book as everything in the box. It's time we put it together.

TOOLS NEEDED FOR THIS BOOK (NOT INCLUDED)

Blank notebook, pencil or pen, index cards, markers, a word processor on a computer, your imagination, and your sense of humor are all you need!

You should also have a secret desire to make people laugh, make a lot of money, and induce massive regret for those who would not date you in high school. As for those unenlightened few (or, in my case, many) who scorned you in high school, we are not going to throw this book at them. It's a trade paperback not a hardback, so it would not cause that much damage — except maybe an angry ouch. And also, it's wrong.

Please only use this book for the power of good, not evil. You are going to use it to write that great screenplay, that comedy blockbuster. That is the best instrument of revenge.

Wait, so that's why people write comedy — for revenge? No, not at all, but chances are, if you are like me, you developed a sense of humor as a defense mechanism. I was a skinny kid with a big nose living on Staten Island with a significant number of cro-magnons. You know how you keep the cro-magnons from beating you up? Make them laugh. And then run really fast.

This book will teach you how to use that sense of humor to make some dollars and cents — that is, how to write a comedy blockbuster.

The best way to use this book is to... hold on to your hat here... read it. From beginning to end. Read the book. Wow. You need a chapter to tell me this? Yes, I want you to read the book and absorb the material on the first read.

There are three main parts of this book. In the first part, you read about the history of film comedy and the various subgenres. As you read about the movies, target some of the movies you find funny. During this section you should start getting an idea of the comedies you like to watch; or, more specifically, the kind you wish you had written. The keys here are "getting an idea." Good ideas take time. They're like seeds. You have to plant them, water them, let 'em grow. Ever bite into a popcorn kernel that hadn't popped? It tastes terrible and hurts your teeth. Comedy ideas that are not fully realized are unpopped kernels. You need to let them sit there a while until they pop. While you are reading about the great history of film comedies, watch some great film comedies. So while READING the first part of the book, you should WATCH these movies.

The second part of the book — and the main idea behind it — is the exploration of the *inappropriate goal* and specifically what goes into the writing of a comedy blockbuster.

If You Are a Starting a Comedy Screenplay...

Start from the beginning. Open a computer file. Read each chapter. Do the exercises and develop your "scriptment" as we move along. Think of this book like a video game — don't go to the next level until you have completed each one.

If Your Have Already Written a Screenplay and Are Stuck in Development Hell...

If you're smart enough to get stuck in development hell, good for you. There are worse places in hell to be. But you do want to get out of there and it's very hard to climb out of hell with the weight of studio notes. Use this book as a roadmap.

Also, if you are using this book for academic purposes, assign one chapter a week, screen the films mentioned in that chapter, and enjoy a dirty martini with the attractive co-ed of your gender-specific choice.

This book was developed as an academic course at the Writer's Program at UCLA. It is structured the same way I have structured my classes. Each chapter is a lecture and a lesson. Have the students do the work and the exercises.

Mostly, to all writers — I encourage you to be fearless, to push the envelope, to teach us to laugh at ourselves and see ourselves for the fools we all are — every day of our lives as we chase our own inappropriate goals.

CHAPTER ONE

HOW TO BUST A GUT

OR COMEDY COLLEGE 101

Everyone thinks he or she is funny. And you've met enough people to know that not everyone is funny. We're going to go forth and attempt to analyze comedy. As E. B. White once put it, "Analyzing humor is like dissecting a frog. Few people are interested and the frog dies of it."

Let's kill some frogs.

I started killing frogs at New York University. I was in the Graduate Film School for Film and Television. I made a very grandiose mafia epic called *Wedding Day*. Nothin' funny about grandiose mafia epics that last twenty minutes. During the screenings of the film in class, I would crack a joke or have a witty comeback. My professor said, "You should put some of that humor in your films."

So my next film was a very grandiose comedy. I loved Robert Zemeckis films, so I tried to make one. It turned out okay. Not great. Okay. Wasn't as funny as I had hoped. But I found out what I loved.

When it was time to write my first feature, I wrote a thriller about a pyschic reporter hot on the trail of a serial killer who turns out to be himself. Wow. Cool stuff. I love cool stuff. *Silence of the Lambs* had just won the Oscar so I figured I would exploit that cash cow and make my way into the business. Juliet (my wife) was a script reader at the newly formed Tribeca Studios in New York City. She was making connections. She was making friends. She got someone to read my script. Art Linson's company was in the same building. He made *The Untouchables.* It was a perfect fit. My script was submitted and I got a great meeting with the development exec, Jill, who sat me down and gave me the most honest notes ever given to me: She called my script derivative.

And she was right. The thriller wasn't in me. It was not part of my D.N.A. I liked to laugh at the world. Not kill people in it. So I tried writing a comedy and that kind of worked out for me.

In my classes people always ask me — can you teach me to be funny?

Ouch.

That's a hard task.

The comedian Larry Miller is purported to have said the following: Here is how you write a joke. You write a joke. You tell the joke. If people laugh, it's funny. If they don't, rewrite the joke.

Seems simple.

Can I really teach you how to write funny? That is an incredibly difficult question to answer: Laughter is not universal. What I find funny might not be funny to you.

Here's what I can teach you — how to think like a comedy writer for motion pictures and long-form television. I can teach you how to be a writer, but not how to write. Kind of like the old Bible quotation: "Give a man a fish, he eats for a day. Teach a man how to fish, he's going to spend a lot of time away from his wife."

A comedy writer needs to be reading funny, thinking funny, writing funny, and watching funny.

The first thing is to write down: What makes you laugh? Is there a particular comic strip you love? Are you more of a *New Yorker* kind of person? Do you like farce? Spoof?

How to read funny

Write down five authors who make you laugh — or at least have made you smile. Read them. Reread them.

How to think funny

Surround yourself with funny people. Simple as that. Join a comedy improv group or take a class. You will meet other funny people. Try stand-up, or start going to stand-up clubs. There are a lot of comedy writing teams out there. You know why? If you can make the other person in the room laugh, chances are it's going to be funny on the page.

Write funny

This book is designed to guide you through the creation of your comedy blockbuster. But like anything else, practice makes perfect. You write and then you rewrite. Think of it like baseball. If a hitter in baseball fails seven out of ten times, he's a very good player. You need to start thinking the same way. Failure *is* an option. The more you do it, the easier it is going to get. You will develop a set of comic muscles.

There is no substitute for writing every day!

Chances are, if you do that, you will succeed. Your work will improve dramatically. Wait, I mean improve comically!

How to watch funny

What's funny? Or, more importantly: What's a funny movie? My first advice is: You should have a decent idea of what is funny before setting off on a journey to write a comedy blockbuster.

I always implore (yes, I'm good at imploring my students) to KNOW THEIR GENRE.

What does this mean?

If you're writing a thriller, you should know the work of Alfred Hitchcock or even Fritz Lang.

If you're writing a western, I hope you've see *Shane.* And the films of John Ford. And you better check out *The Unforgiven.*

The same is true for comedy. Too often I have students who don't know enough about movies.

Now, I don't expect you to stop reading now and start watching every comedy out there from the beginning of celluloid.

But you need to have comedic references from which to draw. I am a big believer that if nothing's going in, nothing's going out.

Comedies tend to be *topical.* They deal with a situation, a mood, something in the zeitgeist. It might be an antiwar comedy like *M.A.S.H.* or a comedy about the birth control pill. Yes, there was one made. Check it out. It starred David Niven. It was called *Prudence and the Pill.*

So now, I wish to present to you:

A CRIMINALLY BRIEF HISTORY OF FILM COMEDY

THE SILENTS

Before it was a cable channel, Nickelodeon was a place people would go to watch movies. Little shorts. Little silent movies. Do you remember the names of the great dramatic actors of the silent era? Okay, go to the front of the class if you said Douglas Fairbanks or Rudolph Valentino. Chances are you said Charlie Chaplin or Buster Keaton. Yes, these guys ruled the day in terms of film comedy.

THE SCREENING ROOM

Charlie Chaplin's Mutual Films, *The Kid, The Gold Rush*
Buster Keaton, *The General, Sherlock Jr.*

There was a great Woody Allen movie, years ago, called *The Purple Rose of Cairo*. A character from a movie walks off the screen and becomes real. Woody Allen cited Keaton's *Sherlock Jr.* as one of his inspirations. *Borat* has moments where the Borat character seems like a direct descendent of Chaplin's Tramp character.

THE SCREWBALL COMEDIES

The Depression hit America in 1929. Money was out. Laughter was in. Many film scholars regard the 1930s as the golden age of film comedy. It was the age of "screwball." Screwball comedy was defined by mistaken identities, frenetic pacing, fast-talking woman not afraid to flaunt their moxie and sexuality, and great leading men not afraid to be the butt of jokes.

Screwball comedy also has great peripheral characters. Other characters in the story are often as funny and zany as the leads. If you want to write film comedy, you need to watch some screwball comedies of the 1930s. There is no wasted space.

Plus, screwball is about something. We'll talk more about this later when we get to *Hilarity and Heart*. The writers of these stories had something to say about the human condition.

The comedy directors of that time were Howard Hawks, Frank Capra, Leo McCarey, Ernest Lubitsch, and Preston Sturges.

The writers were Ben Hecht, Charles McArthur, Billy Wilder, Preston Sturges, and Robert Riskin.

The screwball era continued past the 1930s but it was at its absolute peak when *It Happened One Night* won the grand slam at the Academy Awards in 1934 by taking home

Best Picture, Best Actor, Best Actress, Best Director and, of course, Best Screenplay.

THE SCREENING ROOM

There are a lot of screwball comedies you should watch. I suggest you start with these five:

It Happened One Night

Sullivan's Travels

*His Girl Friday**

The Philadelphia Story

Bringing Up Baby

*Hollywood has always loved remakes. *His Girl Friday* had been filmed before. It is based on the play *The Front Page*. The original story is about two male reporters. Hawks decided to change one of the leads to a woman, and played the whole script with rapid-fire dialogue.

SIDE NOTE: SO YOU REALLY WANT TO DIRECT?

Then write some funny scripts and say you want to direct them! It's that easy, no? Chances are if executives think you're funny on the page, you might be funny behind the camera. Plus there is a precedent that extends for almost a hundred years.

Preston Sturges was the pioneer for the comedy writer/director. After working on five features, he sold his screenplay *The Great McGinty* to Paramount for $1 with the agreement that he would direct it. He not only directed the movie, but he also won the Oscar for Best Screenplay.

Billy Wilder was the co-writer (with Charles Brackett) on the classic screwball comedies *Ninotchka* and *Ball of Fire & Midnight*. He began his illustrious directing career with the movie *The Major and the Minor*.

Woody Allen emerged as a writer/director in 1969 with the "mockumentary" (see genres) *Take the Money and Run*. A few years later, *Annie Hall* became one of the rare comedies to win the Oscar for Best Picture.

John Hughes parlayed his success in writing the screenplay for *National Lampoon's Vacation* into becoming the king of 1980s teen comedies beginning in 1984 with *Sixteen Candles*.

James L. Brooks went from the small screen to the big screen directing the dramatic adaptation of *Terms of Endearment* (1983), following it up four years later with *Broadcast News* (1987). Prior to that he had written the romantic comedy *Starting Over.*

The Farrelly Brothers had never directed a movie before *Dumb and Dumber* in 1994. The legend is they were tired of not seeing their material made so they decided to direct it themselves. No one ever asked them if they had directed before.

In 2005, Judd Apatow scored with *The 40-Year-Old Virgin.*

FILM COMEDY IN THE 1940S

In the 1940s the screwball era was slowing down and audiences became focused on World War II. While *Citizen Kane* came out in 1941 and would go on to be regarded as one of the greatest movies of all time, the box office was dominated by the comedy stylings of vaudeville and radio stars Abbott and Costello in *Buck Privates,* a comedic take on life in the army. They would go on to star in *Abbott and Costello Meet Frankenstein, Abbott and Costello Meet the Invisible Man,* and *Abbott and Costello Meet the Killer.* The horror comedy was born!

Meanwhile, Bob Hope and Bing Crosby were breaking the fourth wall with their "road" movies: *Road to Morocco, Road to Utopia,* and *Road to Rio.* Bob Hope would also star on his own in *My Favorite Blonde* and *My Favorite Brunette.* Hollywood has always loved sequels.

The decade nears the end with the battle of the sexes comedy *Adam's Rib* (1949) starring Spencer Tracey and Katherine Hepburn.

THE SCREENING ROOM

I Married A Witch
Miracle on 34th Street
Abbott and Costello Meet Frankenstein
Adam's Rib

1950S: GO BIG

In the 1950s television found a home in America's living room. The TV dinner was invented. *I Love Lucy* ruled the day. Comedy played very well on television. Sid Caesar was just as big. How could he not be? His writing staff was crammed with future comedy screenwriters: Mel Brooks, Carl Reiner, Larry Gelbart, and Neil Simon. To combat the small screen, Hollywood went big. Big, as in Charlton Heston Big. Large event movies like *The Ten Commandments, Ben Hur,* and *Giant* ruled the box office.

The decade began with Spencer Tracy in *Father of the Bride.* The Battle of the Sexes continued on the screen with movies like *Pat and Mike.* Jerry Lewis and Dean Martin starred in many unmemorable movies. Lewis would break up with Martin and come into his own in the 1960s.

Billy Wilder put Jack Lemmon and Tony Curtis in drag in 1959 in *Some Like it Hot.* Ten years prior, Cary Grant was in drag for *I Was A Male War Bride.* Grant would continue to be box office gold, appearing in *Monkey Business, House Boat,* and *Operation Petticoat.* Rock Hudson would be deemed the next Cary Grant. His comic timing was wonderfully displayed in the Academy Award-winning *Pillow Talk.* Hmm, a *Pillow Talk* update with Twitter?

Remember how I said that comedy is topical — how it's very *in the now*? *Pillow Talk* is a movie about party lines. That is, when you used a phone someone else in your building might be using the same telephone line. They might even listen in on your phone call.

THE SCREENING ROOM

Father of the Bride
Some Like It Hot
Pillow Talk

THE SWINGING 1960s

It was called the "Swinging Sixties" for a reason. As the world went through tumultuous, defining cultural shifts, so did the movies. A generation battled in living rooms across America; the same was happening on the big screen. Studios pumped out Doris Day comedies (*Lover Come Back, That Touch of Mink, The Glass Bottom Boat*) and large ensemble old-fashioned comedies like *It's A Mad, Mad, Mad, Mad World* and *The Great Race.* They were old-fashioned. They didn't really deal with any topical issues. In an era of civil rights, free love, and disenfranchised youth, some comedies became edgier. *Guess Who's Coming to Dinner* is a comedy about a young white woman who brings her black boyfriend home to dinner to meet her very white dad. The seminal comedy of the 1960s might be *The Graduate* (1967) in which young Ben has an affair with Mrs. Robinson and then woos her daughter.

Jerry Lewis enjoyed box office success as a triple threat writer/star/director with movies like *Cinderfella, The Errand Boy,* and *The Nutty Professor.* Underappreciated, Jerry Lewis also invented the video assist so directors could see what was being filmed as it was filmed and he taught filmmaking at University of Southern California film school where, allegedly, George Lucas was one of his students. Maybe this explains Jar-Jar Binks.

One year later, the ratings system created the R-Rating and thus introduced the world to the R-Rated Comedy. Comedy censorship that had been governed by the Hays Code since 1930 was stripped away.

THE SCREENING ROOM

That Touch of Mink

The Graduate

1970s: Pushing the Envelope

On television, *Saturday Night Live* premiered, and tomorrow's comedy movie stars were born: Chevy Chase, John Belushi, Bill Murray, Dan Aykroyd, Jane Curtain, and Gilda Radner. The pattern of comedy stars emerging from SNL continues to this day, with Tina Fey and Kristin Wiig leading the current generation.

Another comedy star to emerge from television was Goldie Hawn. Hawn made the jump from *Laugh In* to box office star with *There's a Girl in My Soup* with Peter Sellars of Pink Panther fame, *Shampoo*, and *Foul Play*.

Meanwhile, the rating code allowed film comedy to become broader and naughtier, with more F-Bombs, nudity, and raunchiness. *M.A.S.H.* was an edgy comedy set against the backdrop of the Korean war and featured guys peeping on the girls' shower. *Shampoo* was a political comedy set against the backdrop of the Nixon election and featured a hairdresser pretending to be gay. *National Lampoon's Animal House* helped college enrollment and informed America about how to throw a good toga party. Everything was fair game in the movies. Lots of tops came off.

Remember those TV writers from the 1950s? They come of age in the 1970s.

Carl Reiner directs Steve Martin in *The Jerk*. He directs *Oh, God!*

Mel Brooks writes and directs *Young Frankenstein*. He is nominated for an Oscar for Best Original Screenplay.

Neil Simon, the amazingly successful playwright of *The Odd Couple,* is nominated for an Oscar for his best original screenplay for *The Goodbye Girl.*

Larry Gelbart is nominated for an Oscar for his adapted screenplay for *Oh, God!*

Woody Allen owned the 1970s: From the broad futuristic *Sleeper* and winning Best Picture with *Annie Hall* to *Manhattan.*

THE SCREENING ROOM
Monty Python and the Holy Grail!
The Jerk
American Graffiti
The In-Laws
A New Leaf

MATERIALISTIC 1980S: LOOSEN UP YUPPIES!

The age of the yuppie! Money was made. Money was lost. And most of the time characters on the screen were making or losing it. Paul Mazursky remakes the classic French film *Boudu Saved From Drowning,* turning it into a contemporary indictment of the rich with *Down and Out in Beverly Hills.*

In *Trading Places,* a rich man (Dan Aykroyd) and a poor man (Eddie Murphy) are forced to switch places. In the end, they team up and turn the tables to bankrupt the greedy billionaires who put them in this mess.

Risky Business was Tom Cruise's break-out movie. He played a teenager who turns his home into a brothel. Not only did he get the girl, but he also got the money to fix his dad's car and buy back his family's "egg" — and he gets into Princeton!

John Hughes wrote and directed the classic *Planes, Trains and Automobiles,* in which an uptight yuppie played by Steve Martin is stuck on the road with a crazy salesman played by the late, great John Candy. Years later, *Due Date* would mine this same comic river.

John Hughes was also responsible for the rise of the teen comedies. *Ferris Bueller's Day Off* touches on the idea that money can't buy you happiness, but most of the teen comedies dealt with real teen issues — love, alienation, cliques. From *Sixteen Candles* and *Pretty in Pink* to *The Breakfast Club*. During his free time, Hughes was able to write *National Lampoon's Vacation* and *National Lampoon's European Vacation*.

The romantic comedy began its resurgence toward the end of the decade with *Moonstruck* and *When Harry Met Sally*. This trend would continue into the 1990s.

THE SCREENING ROOM

Back to the Future
Bull Durham
Ghostbusters
Airplane!
Splash

1990s COMEDIES — GROSS!

Cable explodes. The Internet expands. The gross-out comedy comes into vogue. A remake of *The Shop Around the Corner*, *You've Got Mail* is the iconic AOL email greeting and a movie with Tom Hanks and Meg Ryan. Meg Ryan is America's sweetheart, with *Sleepless in Seattle*, *You've Got Mail*, *I.Q.*, and *French Kiss*.

Julia Roberts will run neck and neck as box office champion with her string of rom-coms: *Pretty Woman, My Best Friend's Wedding, Notting Hill,* and *Runaway Bride*.

Saturday Night Live continues to produce lower ratings on television but huge stars on the big screen. Adam Sandler hits it big with *Wedding Singer*. Bill Murray stars in *What*

About Bob? and the now-appreciated *Groundhog Day*. Dana Carvey and Mike Myers will turn *Wayne's World*, a *Saturday Night Live* sketch, into a successful franchise.

Jim Carrey becomes the champion of big, broad, outlandish comedies. Beginning with *Ace Ventura: Pet Detective*, Carrey enjoys a decade of success as America's box office champ with *The Mask, Dumb & Dumber, Liar, Liar,* and his portrayal of comedian Andy Kaufman in *Man on the Moon*.

Behind the camera, the Farrelly Brothers proved just as funny — and even more outrageous! Never ones to shy away from a disgusting, over-the-top, laugh-invoking sight gag (zipper scene anyone?), the Farrelly Brothers will write and direct *Dumb & Dumber*, the underappreciated *Kingpin,* and the classic *There's Something About Mary*.

The four quadrant movie hits. Four quadrant movies are designed to appeal to men and women over and under twenty-five years old. I think of them as movies that parents as well as their kids will enjoy. *Home Alone* becomes one of the biggest comedy blockbusters of all time.

THE SCREENING ROOM
City Slickers
Four Weddings and a Funeral
Office Space
The Big Lebowski

Y2K: Who Let the Boys Out?

The ladies got off to a good lead in the early 2000s. Reese Witherspoon burst onto the scene with *Legally Blonde* and continued the rom-com success with *Sweet Home Alabama*. Sandra Bullock, who had success in the 1990s with *While You Were Sleeping*, rebounds with *Miss Congeniality.* But then the boys began to rule the day. The romantic comedy shifts to the man's point of view. Helped by a strong crew of male comic actors and their frat-like determination to help each other succeed, the *man-com* is born.

From *Meet the Parents, Wedding Crashers,* and *Forgetting Sarah Marshall* to *Knocked Up* — the question is: Will the man grow up? Will he find love?

The comedies of the male-driven late 2000s featured a group of male comedians appearing in each others' movies, most of the time R-Rated comedies.

- Jack Black in *School of Rock*
- Jack Black, Robert Downey, Jr., and Ben Stiller in *Tropic Thunder*
- Ben Stiller in *Meet the Parents* with Owen Wilson
- Ben Stiller and Vince Vaughn in *Dodgeball*
- Vince Vaughn and Owen Wilson in *Wedding Crashers*
- Vince Vaughn, Luke Wilson, and Will Ferrell in *Old School*
- Will Ferrell in *Anchorman* with Steve Carrell and Paul Rudd
- Steve Carell in *The 40-Year-Old Virgin* with Paul Rudd and Seth Rogan
- Seth Rogan in *Knocked Up* with Jason Segal
- Jason Segel in *I Love You, Man* with Paul Rudd
- Jason Segel in *Forgetting Sarah Marshall* with Jonah Hill and Russell Brand
- Jonah Hill and Russell Brand in *Get Him to the Greek*

But the ultimate box office, R-Rated comedy, the winner and still champ (sorry, Mike Tyson) featured none of those guys: It was *The Hangover.*

So what comes after the man-child? Well, lots of female-driven R-Rated comedies have sold. (See "The R-Rated Woman"). Girls want to prove they can be as raunchy as boys.

Or, chances are, it's something that hasn't been written yet. At least not until you finish this book.

Yes, But What Kind of Comedy?

You're at a party. You tell someone you're writing a comedy. Great, that's all you need to tell them. But you need to be a little more specific in your writing.

Comedy is really how you see the world. Woody Allen made an interesting film in 2004 entitled *Melinda and Melinda*. Here's the premise: A group of writers hear the same story and one decides it's a drama, the other sees it as a comedy.

You see everything as a comedy.

Hollywood has, too. It has taken every genre and turned it on its head. As you begin thinking about your comedy blockbuster, think about what subgenre it might exist in. Here's a few to get you started:

The Subgenres of Comedy

Farce

Farce is defined as a light, humorous play in which the plot depends upon a skillfully exploited situation rather than upon the development of character. So we're not talking anything deep. Farce is weaker on character development. It is superficial — but it can be very funny.

Some classic farce movies include Woody Allen's *Everything You Wanted to Know About Sex (But Were Afraid to Ask)*. This film of the early seventies, featuring a giant rampaging boob, was actually based on a nonfiction sexual reference book written by Dr. David Reuben.

Mel Brooks is a filmmaker who specialized in farce. From skewering Westerns in *Blazing Saddles* (and breaking down the fourth wall) to having Frankenstein dance — in one of the most famous scenes in film history in the classic *Young Frankenstein.*

The *Scary Movie* franchise was a farce loosely based on the *Scream* movie franchise. *Airplane!,* the Zucker-Abrahams-Zucker Brothers classic, was a farce based on a movie called *Zero Hour.*

YOU ALSO GOTTA SEE: *Duck Soup, Blazing Saddles, Hot Shots!*

SEX COMEDY

Sex sells. Sex comedies became more in vogue and more popular with the emergence of the rating code. But sex comedies are not just about naked foreplay. They always are, as comedies are, reflective of the time and the environment around them.

One of the first sex comedies was the 1969 Paul Mazursky film, *Bob & Carol & Ted & Alice,* in which close friends decide to go to Vegas to have an orgy. Judd Apatow and Steve Carell's *The 40-Year-Old Virgin* is a must-see sex comedy. The character was born on the improv stage.

Please note: Both these movies have very mature endings. The protagonists realize there is more to life than the pursuit of sex and find this funny little thing called love in the end. Both movies end in song. *Bob & Carol & Ted & Alice* ends with "What the World Needs Now" (is love sweet love). *The 40-Year-Old Virgin* ends with Andy (Carell) singing "The Age of Aquarius."

YOU ALSO GOTTA SEE: *10, The Sure Thing, Superbad*

Teen Comedy

Teen comedies have been a mainstay of comedy since Mickey and Judy wanted to put on a show, or Frankie and Annette hung out in *Beach Blanket Bingo*. A recent addition is *American Pie*, which follows the adventures of three teens determined to lose their virginity. Even more recently, *Superbad* follows the adventures of teens with the same goal.

But it's not always about sex. Regardless of what parents believe their teens are thinking about — it's not always about sex. They are dealing with real issues — identity, expectations, the social hierarchy in high school. And no one was ever better at talking to a generation than the late, great John Hughes. In 1985, he made *The Breakfast Club*, a film about five teens from very different cliques — stoner, jock, brain, princess, and social misfit — who are sentenced to detention on a Saturday and learn (as we do) that there is much more going on than we realize.

YOU ALSO GOTTA SEE: *Fast Times at Ridgemont High, The Girl Next Door*

Romantic Comedy

Romantic comedies (or Rom-Coms) have been the heart and soul of comedy blockbusters. They are the perfect date night movie. A couple goes to see a movie about a couple falling in love — along the way they bicker, argue, break-up, and (most of the time) get back together.

Annie Hall with Woody Allen and Diane Keaton is a romantic comedy where the couples do not wind up together. Almost thirty years later, *The Break-Up* explored similar thematic territory with Vince Vaughn and Jennifer Aniston.

From *It Happened One Night* and *Roman Holiday* to *The Proposal*, men and woman have long been going at it on the screen so they can go at it in the bedroom. Each has a clear point of view that grates on the other, but they are still attracted to each other.

Pretty Woman was one of the break-out comedies of the 1990s. It made Julia Roberts into a star. It was your typical rich-man-hires-hooker-and-falls-in-love movie. Sure doesn't sound like comedic material. Originally it wasn't. The script by J. F. Lawton was entitled *3,000*. It was dark and gritty and ended with the rich man tossing the hooker back onto the street. Legend has it that studio chief Jeffrey Katzenberg decided it could be a comedy. He was right.

Traditionally, romantic comedies were told from the woman's point of view. That has changed in the Age of Apatow (Judd, that is) as we see in movies like *Knocked* Up.

YOU ALSO GOTTA SEE: *When Harry Met Sally, Bridget Jones's Diary, Four Weddings and a Funeral*

Action Comedy

Lights. Action. Comedy! Guns. Explosions. Spies. Things that go boom can blow up in laughter. James Cameron of *Avatar* and *Terminator* did all these things for laughs in *True Lies*, a remake of the French action comedy *La Totale.*

Midnight Run was about an accountant and bounty hunter on the run from the mob.

Mr. and Mrs. Smith with Brad Pitt and Angelina Jolie took the battle of the sexes to new heights as the married assassins tried to kill each other. Talk about thematic!

YOU ALSO GOTTA SEE: *Tropic Thunder, Beverly Hills Cop, Smoky and the Bandit*

Sports Comedy

Guys love sports. Guys love comedy. It's a total peanut butter-and-chocolate moment. Perfect together ever since Harold Lloyd ran for a touchdown in *The Freshman.*

Do you have a *Bad News Bears* in you? If you want realism in sports comedies, take a look at the movies of Ron Shelton. Shelton actually played minor league baseball. It sure shows in *Bull Durham*, although his comedic realism was also on display in *Tin Cup* and *White Men Can't Jump*.

Paul Newman's foray into comedy — and you just thought he would be remembered for serious fare and salad dressing — was the classic hockey comedy *Slapshot*.

Caddyshack is a classic comedy about golf! *Dodgeball* is a comedy about dodgeball! *The Mighty Ducks* is the Bad News Bears on ice!

What sport do you love? Did you play field hockey, rugby, lacrosse, Ultimate Frisbee? Is there a movie there?

YOU ALSO GOTTA SEE: *Major League, Kingpin, The Longest Yard*

Boy's Club

Comedies will sometimes center around a group of guys and the trouble they get themselves into. Boy's club movies give us a view into the psyche of the male mind. Boys will be boys. They will drink. Avoid commitment. Fight.

Barry Levinson's *Diner* offers a nostalgic look at the 1950s and features an amazing cast of male stars. *National Lampoon's Animal House* is the ultimate boy's club as we witness life inside the worst fraternity ever to be shown on screen. Years later, *Old School* will feature three men who yearn for their "Animal House" days, so they start a fraternity.

Swingers was the breakout movie for Jon Favreau, Vince Vaughn, and Doug Liman. It's about a group of guys hanging in Los Angeles chasing honeys.

YOU ALSO GOTTA SEE: *The Hangover, Boys Night Out, Stripes*

GIRL'S CLUB

In recent years the girls have been knocking on the door — loudly. And audiences are letting them. Girls love to have fun, too. *Where the Boys Are* is a classic comedy about four girls heading down to Florida for spring break. The *Sex in The City* franchise is the ultimate girl's club. What does a movie need to be a girl's club movie? It needs to be a movie from the female point of view, like *Romy and Michele's High School Reunion* or *Boys On the Side*. *Bridesmaids* just took the prize!

YOU ALSO GOTTA SEE: *The Banger Sisters, Outrageous Fortune, The Sweetest Thing.*

MOCKUMENTARY

Ah, the Beatles. Those amazing boys from Liverpool were not just musicians — they were actors, comedic actors inspired by the Marx Brothers. Under director Richard Lester's tutelage, the Beatles played themselves in their debut movie, *A Hard Day's Night*. The plot of the movie follows four days in the life of the Beatles. And thus, the mockumentary was born. But it really grew up five years later when Woody Allen wrote and directed a fictional documentary about a small-time criminal entitled *Take the Money and Run*. A mockumentary treats its subject matter as if it is real; it often has a voice over, and gives the audience members an overview of the lives or events of their generation. And, of course, the subject of the mockumentary is absurd.

YOU ALSO GOTTA SEE: *This is Spinal Tap, Borat, Best in Show, CB4*

STONER COMEDIES

Reefer Madness is not a stoner comedy, though it plays like one. Made in the 1950s, this B film shows the terrible effects of marijuana. Stoner comedies show the comical effects of marijuana. They came of age in the 1970s. It was time for that free love, hippie generation to make it on the screen. The Stoner Comedy godfathers were the comedians Cheech Martin and Tommy Chong. In 1978, they rolled across America in their car made of pot in *Up in Smoke*. Drugs have always been prevalent in comedies — but stoner comedies tend to be about the pursuit of drugs or guys and gals on drugs in the pursuit of something else — say a White Castle Hamburger in *Harold and Kumar Go To White Castle*. For a while, Hollywood became very conservative and stoner comedies were no longer being made. It was more acceptable to make movies about very stupid people (*Dumb & Dumber*) than very stoned people.

YOU ALSO GOTTA SEE: *Pineapple Express, Up In Smoke, Harold and Kumar Go To White Castle*

FANTASY/MAGIC

Magic can be funny. From the time Fredric March had to tangle with a witch in *I Married A Witch,* magic and fantasy have been major components of film comedy.

A studio exec will always ask: What are the rules? What is the device that causes the magic? A recurring theme of this subgenre is "Be careful what you wish for."

YOU ALSO GOTTA SEE: *Big, Groundhog Day.*

GOD COMEDIES

Anything to do with God and heaven and angels falls into the category of God Comedies. From the original *Heaven Can Wait,* entitled *Here Comes Mr. Jordan,* to Clarence in *It's A Wonderful Life* to Nora Ephron's *Michael,* angels are often sent to Earth to interact with characters in need of spirituality. And if that isn't enough, sometimes God interacts.

In the 1970s, George Burns got to play God in the hit movie *Oh, God!* in which he comes to Earth and asks poor John Denver to deliver his message. Years later, Jim Carrey got very angry at God and thought he could do a better job, so God (Morgan Freeman) gave him a shot in the movie *Bruce Almighty*.

YOU ALSO GOTTA SEE: *It's A Wonderful Life, We're No Angels*

CRIME

Stick 'em up! Reach for the skies! Is that a gun in your pocket or are you just happy to see me? America has been laughing at crime since movies began. Crime movies might be about losers or the desperate trying to pull off a crime (*Bottle Rocket, Small Town Crooks*) or criminals dealing with an unseen complication in their criminal plans (*The Lady Killers*). *48 Hours* was a buddy crime movie about a cop and a criminal teamed up for 48 hours. It is a "must see" movie for witnessing the arrival of Eddie Murphy as the new sheriff in town.

A Fish Called Wanda is a crime caper. Complications ensue when Jamie Lee Curtis falls in love with barrister Archibald Leach (John Cleese.) Side note: Archibald Leach is Cary Grant's real name.

YOU ALSO GOTTA SEE: *Lavender Hill Mob, Bad Boys, Beverly Hills Cop, Take the Money and Run*

MOB COMEDY

Americans love to laugh at the Mafia's expense… at least in the safety of their own home or in a darkened theater. We are either focusing on the fish out of water who gets involved with the mob (*Analyze This*), or the mob that gets involved in the very ordinary world (*Get Shorty, Bullets over Broadway*). Though *Some Like It Hot* featured a major mob plot device and antagonist (played by George Raft, who allegedly had a real criminal background), most mob comedies appeared post-*The Godfather.*

YOU ALSO GOTTA SEE: *The Whole Nine Yards, Married to the Mob, Prizzi's Honor*

WAR

War is hell. And it is never played just for laughs. But war is also absurd. And movie comedies have shown us how absurd it can be. From *Catch-22* to *Dr. Strangelove, or How I Learned to Stop Worrying and Love the Bomb,* war comedies show us either how insane war is or how people cope with war.

YOU ALSO GOTTA SEE: *M.A.S.H, Good Morning, Vietnam*

BIOGRAPHY A.K.A BIO-COMS

In recent years, screenwriters Scott Alexander and Larry Karaszewski have owned the bio-com. It might be because they invented it. From *Ed Wood* to *Man on the Moon*, Alexander and Karasewski have found real-life characters who border on the absurd.

YOU ALSO GOTTA SEE: *Man On The Moon, Private Parts, Ed Wood*

CULTURE COMS

The success of Spike Lee's *She's Gotta Have It* opened the door for African-American-centric comedies. Ranging from the broad (*Booty Call*) and Tyler Perry's movies to movies like *The Wood* or *Just Wright*, these comedies are defined by their very specific cultural points of view. In the same way, *Moonstruck* is a comedy about the Italian-American culture and way of life and *Tortilla Soup* is a comedy about Latino culture, these films provide a comedic window onto their specific worlds.

YOU ALSO GOTTA SEE: *Lottery Ticket, My Big Fat Greek Wedding*

ALT-COMS — COMEDIES ABOUT ALT LIFESTYLES

Hollywood is always late to the party. Despite the fact that Hollywood is an industry that is very open to different lifestyles, independent filmmakers broke the mold on comedies about alternative lifestyle choices. Ang Lee would go on to direct the mainstream, Oscar-winning *Brokeback Mountain,* but he started with the independent and critically received comedy *The Wedding Banquet.* In the 1990s, after years of independent movies, Alt-Coms went mainstream with alternative lifestyles at the center of the story with *In & Out,* in which Kevin Kline plays a high school drama teacher about to be married who is outed on national TV; and *The Birdcage,* a remake of the Veber French classic, *La Cage aux Folles.*

YOU ALSO GOTTA SEE: *Kissing Jessica Stein, Billy Hollywood's Screen Test, Kiss Me, Guido*

HORROR

Ever since Bob Hope battled ghosts in *Ghostbreakers,* audiences have loved a good laugh and a good scream. This hybrid has made fun of Dracula (*Love at First Bite*), werewolves (*Teen Wolf*), zombies *(Shaun of the Dead),* and more ghosts (*Ghostbusters*)

YOU ALSO GOTTA SEE: *American Werewolf in London, Young Frankenstein, Witches of Eastwick.*

SATIRE

How does one define satire? It's a genre that takes a dark, comical look at a serious but absurd subject. It uses irony and sarcasm to denounce a situation or a view. It can be about politics, the news media, war, or even marriage. Satire always seems very grounded in reality. In the classic movie *Being There,* Peter Sellers plays a dim-witted gardener who becomes a political confidant and possibly the next President of the United States. Everyone interprets what he says as metaphor. The audience is in on the joke but the characters in the movie simply don't get it. *Wag the Dog* satirizes the news media's coverage of wars. Paddy Chayefsky skewered the outrageousness of network news reporting in 1976 in the classic movie *Network*. Unfortunately, what he was condemning is even more prevalent today.

YOU ALSO GOTTA SEE: *Thank You For Smoking, To Die For, War of the Roses*

Musical Comedy

A tradition on Broadway, the original musical comedy left the screen for a while. For a primer on what makes people laugh, see the 1952 musical *Singin' in the Rain*. Hollywood tends to film what worked on Broadway (*The Producers*). There is hope on the smaller screen; on the Internet *Dr. Horrible's Sing-Along Blog* became a huge hit.

YOU ALSO GOTTA SEE: *Grease, The Producers, A Funny Thing Happened On the Way to the Forum*

Sidenote: Remember those TV writers who succeeded on the big screen? Well, *The Producers* was written by Mel Brooks and *A Funny Thing Happened on the Way to the Forum* was written for the stage by the late, great Larry Gelbart.

Science Fiction

Do you want to take jokes where no jokes have gone before? Comedies have been out of this world since movies began. From *Abbott and Costello Go to Mars* to *Men in Black*, comedies have combined the high adventure of speculative fiction with out-and-out belly aches.

YOU ALSO GOTTA SEE: *Galaxy Quest, Men in Black*

● EXERCISE: BEG, STEAL, OR BORROW

We have just gone through the history of film comedy. Start making a list of your **TOP TEN** favorite comedies of all time.

Write them down.

Write down what makes you laugh. Which scene? Which character? Which particular piece of dialogue?

Don't over-analyze. We are working from a gut level here.

Now think about those films. Are there any similiarities? Do they take place in the same setting? Is romance involved? Are they by the same writer? The same director?

Now rent the three movies that have some things in common.

Watch them again. We want to find out what makes you laugh.

CHAPTER TWO

THE COMEDIC IDEA

A.K.A. THE IMPORTANCE OF BEING INAPPROPRIATE A.K.A. THE BLUES BROTHERS ARE NOT ROLE MODELS

The room was filling with suits. Lot of suits. It was a pitch meeting. The most important one of our new career. We were at Universal to pitch our take on the movie version of *Archie*. The studio executive, Carr, had championed us. But now we had to win over the other executives and the producers and... there were a lot of them.

I think there were nine people in the room.

Everyone was looking at us to make them laugh and to tell them a story.

I looked around the quiet room and said: "I'm very confused by all these people here. I'm not sure whose ass I should be kissing right now."

HUGE LAUGH.

It was the inappropriate thing to say at a meeting and I am convinced it was one of the reasons we got the job.

So what does "being inappropriate" mean?

Did you ever fart during dinner?

Did you ever laugh at a funeral?

Did you ever tell a woman that pregnancy makes her look radiant only to have her tell you she is not pregnant?

If conflict is the lifeblood of drama, inappropriate behavior is the lifeblood of comedy.

Scholars have studied *commedia dell'arte* and the comedies of Shakespeare (he wrote some good ones). Inside the comedy blockbusters of those days, you will find some of the comedic plot devices found in screenplays today: deception, mistaken identity, the ongoing battle of the sexes, guys in drag, gals in drag. All of these devices (and we will discuss more as the book goes on) come from the same pot.

There are three main ingredients in your comedic blockbuster recipe:

INAPPROPRIATE GOAL

INAPPROPRIATE BEHAVIOR

INAPPROPRIATE DIALOGUE

By definition, *inappropriate* means not suitable for a particular situation.

We're going to cover behavior and dialogue in the next section (characters). Right now, to build that big comedy blockbuster idea, let's focus on the inappropriate goal.

THE INAPPROPRIATE GOAL

Every movie can be boiled down to the same plot — someone wants something and is having trouble getting it. In the case of comedy — the question is what is the "it?"

Dramas have worthy goals. A British soldier decides he wants to unite Arabia. A divorced man fights his wife for custody of his children.

Mysteries might have the goal: The detective wants to find the killer.

Thrillers might up the stakes: The C.I.A. has to find out where the bomb is hidden before it goes off.

Comedy goals are a little off the wall, or less intense. The goals might be: The teenager needs to get laid; the guys need to get the band back together; we need to crash the wedding. In the recent rom-com *No Strings Attached*, Adam (Ashton Kutcher) and Emma (Natalie Portman) decide to be sex buddies and to use each other. The goal is *not* to fall in love. Very inappropriate for a romantic comedy.

But when something isn't suitable, it's usually funny. In the case of the inappropriate goal, it's two-fold. It's not only funny, but it also fuels our engine for the rest of the story. Inappropriate behavior can lead to outrageous antics.

Sidenote: Just because the goal is inappropriate doesn't mean it's not important. What is happening in the story is the most important event in your main character's life.

For example, in *Tootsie*, Michael Dorsey cannot get work as an actor. It pains him. He has to work to produce a play. But no one will work with him. So he decides to audition for a part as a woman. Dressed in drag, he gets it.

The inappropriate goal is the most important event/action in your story. Everything will emerge from the goal — the logline, characters, plot devices, and resolution.

Let's take a look at the inappropriate goals of some classic comedies.

Risky Business. Consider the teenage hero's inappropriate goal: to start a brothel and pay back a loan shark. Whoa! We're talking about a suburban high school kid who has this goal. Clearly not appropriate! If Tom Cruise wanted to start a lawn mowing business or a car wash business to pay off his debt, that would be earnest, but I don't know how funny it would be.

Following in the footsteps of *Risky Business* about thirty years later, two other movie characters decide to use sex to solve their cash flow problems. I'm referring to *Zack and Miri Make a Porno*. Two best friends are so sunk in debt, they decide that the quickest way out of their financial mess is to make a porno film together. Appropriate? Certainly not. Funny? Yes.

In the recent hit *The Hangover* four friends have gone to Las Vegas for a bachelor party. Sure, we've seen bachelor party movies before. (Tom Hank's *Bachelor Party* and *American Wedding*). They can be R-Rated for obvious reasons and lead to their own inappropriate behavior. But *The Hangover* isn't about having a good time. The characters' goal in the movie is to find the groom. Yes, the groom has disappeared, which is not appropriate behavior for anyone the night before his wedding.

Now, in most romantic comedies, boy wants girl or girl wants boy. Both are reasonable goals. But matters of love are never so appropriate.

In the movie *10*, George Webber (Dudley Moore) falls in love with Jenny Hanley (Bo Derek). Just one small problem: She's just gotten married. In fact, she's still in her wedding dress when he first lays eyes on her! He meets her literally as she's pulling away from the church in a limo with her new husband. But it doesn't stop him on his inappropriate goal as he pursues her on her honeymoon. Now imagine if *10* were about Dudley Moore waffling about whether or not to marry Samantha (Julie Andrews), his long-suffering girlfriend. Not a bad story about commitment phobia. But not close to Blake Edwards's comedic view of one man's mid-life crisis.

In *Tin Cup*, Roy (Kevin Costner) is a washed up golf pro who tries to qualify for the US Open in order to win the heart of Molly (Renee Russo), the girlfriend of Don Johnson, his successful rival. Trying to win a sports event to impress a girl is hardly inappropriate unless she's the girlfriend of your competition. Then it could be seen as inappropriate.

In *There's Something About Mary,* Ted (Ben Stiller) hires a private detective to track down Mary (Cameron Diaz), his high school crush and almost prom date. Clearly, hiring a detective to find a girl to date is not the right way to start a relationship. Trouble and humor are surely going to ensue.

In *Pretty Woman,* Edward Lewis (Richard Gere) hires a prostitute for three days to be his girlfriend. 'Nuff said!

Knowing the inappropriate goal leads us to developing the comedic logline.

THE COMEDIC LOGLINE A.K.A. THE PITCH

In Hollywood, you're always pitching. Always. And a rule of pitching is to reference a movie that succeeded at the box office. I once spent a summer pitching by constantly referencing the hit movie *300.*

It's like *Pretty Woman* meets *300.*

It's like *Stripes* meets *300.* (Actually, that one is not bad).

The point is *300* made a ton of money and the joke always got a laugh in the room.

Pitching is an art form. It's a performance. But you never want to go on too long. I once heard about two writers pitching to a studio executive. (Figure you have about fifteen minutes to pitch your movie). Well, fifteen minutes into this pitch, the writers looked up at the Studio Executive and said: "...and that's the end of the first act."

"No, that's the end of the pitch," the Studio Exec responded and walked out. It can be tough. It can be brutal.

My wife and I were once pitching at Amblin. It's the wonderful bungalow that Steven Spielberg calls home. We meet with the executive in a conference room. She was lovely. Intelligent. And she offered us something to drink. This was Amblin (later known as Dreamworks) — so word on the street was that it had the best drinks. Usually a pitch is the "bottled water tour." You go meeting to meeting collecting bottled water.

This was Steven Spielberg's company! No bottled water here. They had vanilla ice-blended coffee drinks.

Yes, we'll take two! My wife, Juliet (and writing partner at the time) exclaimed. The assistant hustled to get our drinks and we began the pitch.

And it died. In the room. Maybe a sentence or two into the story. Did you ever go to a party and talk to someone you found attractive and wanted to be with? And then you start talking to them and realize they are not interested in you? No way. No how. It is not going to happen. Ever. Why are you even talking to me!?

That's what happened to us at Spielberg's company.

My wife and I wrapped up the pitch. We knew it was dead and not going anywhere.

There was silence. The meeting was over. The ice-blended vanilla drinks had not even arrived.

"What about the drinks?" I asked.

"We have to-go cups," the Exec said.

Holy crap!

And they did.

How many bad pitches had they heard to think, "We have to get some to-go cups in here"?

I can't wait to meet her again and remind her of that story. Call me, Nina!

The truth about pitching is this: I compare it to the old Groucho Marx show where a contestant comes on and if the magic word is said in conversation, a duck drops down holding a placard of the word — and the contestant wins a prize.

If your agenda meets their agenda — you have a chance to sell your pitch.

Which is why you need to have the elevator pitch ready.

Do you know what an elevator pitch is? You're in a building, going to a dentist or visiting a lawyer, and you get in an elevator on the twentieth floor. The elevator stops. A famous, successful movie producer or agent or star gets in the elevator with you. You say hello, and say you love their work and mention that you finished a screenplay.

"What's it about?" the guy or gal asks. (He or she is in a good mood because the pregnancy test came out negative).

You begin talking, rambling, spitting out words like "and then" and "stuff happens," and "I'm not sure"; you spent a long time setting up the story and why you wrote it (WHO CARES!?).

The elevator doors open. The Hollywood guy or gal scrambles away, mumbles "Good luck," and is glad to get out of there.

The elevator pitch is your comedic logline that hints/states your inappropriate goal and can be conveyed in one or two sentences. It should be like the set-up of a good joke. The screenplay that you are going to write is the punch line.

Here is why the logline is so important: You will develop a logline. From that logline, you will develop characters, outline your story, write your screenplay, and rewrite your screenplay. You will hand that screenplay in to an agent. She will love it but will have notes. You will rewrite it some more. The agent will then try to shop the script, putting it out onto the market. It will make it into the hands of a development executive. The exec will love it, and then go into a meeting to convince his or her boss that he must buy this screenplay. The Boss (who is the same guy from the elevator!) will ask,

"What is it about?" The development executive is then going to have to recite the same elevator pitch, the same logline.

Your screenplay will always come full circle back to the logline.

Here are some loglines of comedies that have been purchased over the last few years. See if you can identify the **inappropriate goal** within the logline.

Best Man-A-Thon
When a guy accidentally proposes to his girlfriend, his two best friends hold a competition to be his best man.

Crazy For You
After visiting his grandmother in a mental hospital, an introvert falls for a beautiful nurse and takes her out on a date — only to discover she's not a nurse at all — she's a committed mental patient whom he's accidentally released.

Lovestruck
Two jaded, sarcastic women find themselves trapped in a romantic comedy world.

Eduarrrdo
Superbad-type guys find an ET-like alien in their backyard and help him get home.

The Fresh Man
Faced with the prospect of joining the family port-a-potty business, a slacker with a 1.2 GPA lies his way into college by pretending to be a minority — a female-to-male transsexual.

Untitled Facebook Feature
An awkward ad exec puts a few innocent lies on his Facebook page to make himself sound cooler, but when his exaggerations magically come true, his world is flipped upside down.

Man Up

Josh Mitchell is NOT a guy's guy, so when he finds out that he's having a son, he panics at the mere idea of having to teach him to throw a spiral, hit a curve ball, change a tire, or do pretty much anything manly. To save his unborn son from a life of playground humiliation, Josh begins a crash course in all things "guy" from the manliest man he knows, someone whose teachings he soundly ignored for the last thirty years — his dad.

Jailbait

Two sexually frustrated best friends start dating female prison inmates in hopes of hassle-free relationships complete with conjugal visits, but things become more complicated than they first expect...

The Lay After Tomorrow

Harold and Kumar meets *Bill and Ted.* Two teenagers make a pact to get laid before the world ends.

White House Party

The President's son throws a party in the White House.

The F-Word by Elan Mastai

Two best friends struggle with falling in love without ruining the bond between them.

Bad Teacher by Lee Eisenberg and Gene Stupnitsky

After being dumped by her boyfriend, a foul-mouthed, gold-digging seventh-grade teacher sets her sights on a colleague who is dating the school's model teacher.

Your Dreams Suck by Kat Dennings & Geoffrey Litwak

An awkward teen with no self-esteem regains his self-confidence after joining a Dance Revolution team.

Freshly Popped by Megan Parsons

A teenage girl who works at a movie theater tries to decide to whom she wants to lose her virginity.

The How-To Guide for Saving the World by Ben David Grabinski

A loser discovers a book on how to stop an alien invasion and is thrust into action to stop a real one.

The Most Annoying Man in the World by Kevin Kopelow & Heath Seifert

A man travels across the country with his annoying brother in order to get to his own wedding.

'Til Beth Do Us Part by Jon Hurwitz & Hayden Schlossberg

The friendship of two twenty-something men is put to the test when one of them becomes engaged.

Are you finding the inappropriate goal? Notice the loglines are setting up the story, they are enticing you, seducing you to **read the script**. We are doing something similar now. We are developing a logline so you can **write the script**.

The comedic logline should elicit a chuckle, a laugh, a guffaw. The listener/reader should then be wondering **WHAT HAPPENS NEXT?**

There should be natural curiosity. A comedic question has been raised. What is going to happen to the teen throwing the party in the White House? Are they going to trash the place? Is he going to get in trouble?

Here are some more loglines as compiled by The Black List. *http://blcklst.com/*

As they write on their website:

THE BLACK LIST is a snapshot of the collective taste of the people who develop, produce, and release theatrical feature films in the Hollywood studio system and the mainstream independent system.

An annual list of Hollywood's most liked unproduced screenplays published on the second Friday of December each year, THE BLACK LIST began in 2004 as a survey with contributions from 75 film studio and production company executives. In 2009, over 300 executives contributed their opinion.

Since its inception, dozens of screenplays that appeared on the list have been optioned, produced, and released, many to great commercial success. Two of the top three screenplays on the inaugural 2005 list — *JUNO* by Diablo Cody and *LARS AND THE REAL GIRL* by Nancy Oliver — went on to be nominated for Best Original Screenplay at the 2008 Academy Awards, with JUNO winning the Oscar.

In the loglines below, look for the dramatic, comedic question the logline is raising.

The Oranges by Jay Reiss and Ian Helfer

It's About: Two New Jersey families are thrown into comic turmoil when the prodigal daughter returns for Christmas and falls in love with her parents' best friend.

It's Like: *The Graduate* engaged to *Meet the Parents*.

Status: Anthony Bregman (*Thumbsucker*) and MRC will produce. Julian Farino (*Entourage*) is negotiating to direct.

F***buddies by Liz Meriwether

It's About: Emma and Adam have the best relationship ever! They're twenty-something pals who, you know, do it. A lot. But then Adam goes and falls in love with Emma and ruins everything. Can their perfect nonunion survive?

It's Like: *When Harry Met Sally…* for the *Juno* generation.

Status: Ivan Reitman's company is developing it.

UNIQUELY FAMILIAR

Did you notice that some of the loglines included what movies the script is "like"? When people say it's "like," they are often talking about the tone. *What's the tone?* was a question that befuddled me early on. When I was asked, "What's the tone?" I would say things like broad comedy or psychological thriller. Hollywood doesn't always speak that language. They do in meetings when discussing the particulars of the script. Regardless of what you might think, Hollywood is filled with very smart and very hard working people who are always looking for that next great script.

"What's the tone?" is like speed dating, or speed reading. It quickly categorizes the idea in terms of what kind of comedy it might be. Is it a Farrelly Brothers or a Woody Allen?

There's another reason you want to know the tone, or what movies it might be like: Hollywood studios love ideas that are *uniquely familiar.*

Russell Brand, the very funny, crazy, and the second luckiest man on earth (see Katy Perry), did a remake of the classic Dudley Moore movie, *Arthur.* It's an update of the original. And, as much as I revere Steve Gordon's original, I have to say if you're going to update *Arthur,* Russell Brand seems like a good way to go. He's British, incredibly funny, a daring and honest comedian and performance artist.

But sometimes a remake isn't a direct remake. Russell Brand also made a movie called *Get Him to the Greek* and it kind of reminded me of a classic movie that starred Peter O'Toole called *My Favorite Year.* If you haven't seen *My Favorite Year,* you should. A classic. Very funny. Great one-liners.

Both movies have the same elevator pitch: Hmmm, young impressionable assistant who hasn't learned to live is assigned to babysit an out-of-control legend. Hijinks ensue. There's hilarity and heart (the two essential ingredients to a great comedy).

It seems to be the same story. Now, *My Favorite Year* was close to thirty years ago. I'm not sure how many people at the studio realized they were making something uniquely familiar.

What makes it different? P Diddy? Sex, drugs, rock and roll. Yes, it's R-Rated.

But there's something else that's uniquely familiar about *Get Him to the Greek.* The character Russell Brand is playing first appeared in one of the most original comedies of the last twenty years: Jason Segal's *Forgetting Sarah Marshall.* It featured Russell Brand playing the hysterical Aldous Snow. So Russell Brand is reprising his role as Aldous Snow. But Jonah Hall is playing a character named Aaron Green. In *Forgetting Sarah Marshall,* he played Matthew the Waiter.

So, yes, in some ways *Get Him to the Greek* is an "homage" to *My Favorite Year* but it's more of a vehicle for Aldous Snow.

Let's see if you recognize the plot of another Russell Brand movie that seems uniquely familiar.

Deadline Hollywood recently reported that, "Russell Brand has been cast to star in a film in which he will play a 'David Beckham-like millionaire soccer star/playboy' who gets arrested and must do community service as the soccer coach for a local high school team."

Well, you can say it's *The Bad News Bears* with soccer. Or *The Mighty Ducks* with soccer. Or the *Big Green* with soccer. Wait, didn't that have soccer?

Writers often go to the well looking for that new idea. *Due Date* is a hit. But then so was *Planes, Trains and Automobiles.*

And sometimes that new idea is found in old places… which brings us back to our comedic exercise.

● EXERCISE: TWENTY UNIQUELY FAMILIAR IDEAS

YOUR COMIC LOGLINE

I'm sure you have an idea for a movie. I'm sure you have lots of ideas for a movie. But let's say you don't. You should start developing some. I worked with a manager a few years back who introduced me to the **TWENTY IDEA EXERCISE.**

Managers and agents want to know that you're not a one trick pony. They want to see that you have other ideas. Often they will ask you to send over twenty one-liners. Not all of the one-liners will work. But maybe there's one or two in there worth pursuing.

Here's a little comic exercise you can try. You're going to need a movie guide for this one. By the way, movie guides are one of the most indispensable reference books you can have when first starting out. It's one of those books that list every movie available on DVD. There's always a short logline or elevator pitch of the movie.

Avoid using an on-line database. You want to be able to browse, flip the pages. Discover movies you never knew existed.

Here's what you're going to need: A legal pad, a pen, and that movie guide.

TAKE AN OLD MOVIE AND GIVE IT A TWIST

You can do any combination of the following:

- Change the setting
- Change the genre
- Change the characters

Let's try some. I did this exercise with one of my classes. The only rule was that the end result had to be comedy. Here are some we came up with:

The old movie: *Ferris Bueller's Day Off*.
We change the character of Ferris to a bored mom.
The logline: *Ferris Bueller's Day Off* with a mom
A bored mom decides to cut out for a day and experiences a world of trouble. (*Playdate*)

The old movie: *What About Bob?*
With a woman or ex-girlfriend.
A guy's or gal's ex-girlfriend or friend from college happens back into their lives. (*Remember Gwen*)

The Apartment in a dorm
Loser guy in college is always giving up his dorm room to jocks so they can sleep with co-eds. (*Dorm Room*)

Arthur with a rich party girl who falls in love with a fireman. (*Fire & Ice*)

Parenthood with the in-laws
Following three people who marry into a family. (*The Outlaws*)

The War of the Roses with brothers
Two brothers fight over splitting up a business. (*Brotherly Love*)

Oceans 11 with wives who decide to rob the Super Bowl. (*Huddle*)

All of Me with a divorced couple
Two people switch bodies a week before their second weddings. (*Bride vs. Groom*)

Now it's your turn. Come up with twenty ideas for a comedy. Yes. Twenty! Some will be good; some won't be good. But the more you throw at the wall, the better the chances that something is going to stick!

THE FILL-IN-THE BLANKS ELEVATOR PITCH

Still stuck? Okay, let's go about it a different way. If you're not stuck, then this part is about expanding your idea.

A logline suggests the movie. You want to get people to watch it. It's like looking in a newspaper or a movie guide and seeing what the movie is about. You don't want to know the whole story. You just want to know if you should see the thing.

A logline presents the basics of the story in one sentence, sometimes two. It doesn't dive deep into character.

Sell the sizzle. Make us want to read it.

Oh, and it should make us chuckle. Just a little.

If you're stuck, try plugging information into the following. It's the fill-in-the-blanks game of the LOGLINE.

In the tone of [insert successful or classic movie that made lots of money], [your title] is about a [protagonist, think in terms of character — single dad, stay-at-home mom. disgraced mobster, slacker] who decides to [inappropriate goal] so that he can [what do they want?].

Here's the bad example:

In the tone of *Big, Small* is about a school nerd who is shrunk down to the size of a mouse and gets revenge on everyone who wronged him in school.

REMEMBER: The logline introduces the story, offering a taste of the movie without forcing readers to devour the whole script. As they become familiar with the movie idea, the readers exercise their own imaginations. This hook brings them a step closer to asking to read the script.

CHEAT SHEET

Some logline NEVERS: Don't use cop-out clichés like "mayhem ensues" or "comedy ensues" or "sparks fly," etc.

THE WELL

You have decided to write a screenplay. A better decision might be to make the decision to be a writer. Being a writer means having homework every single day of your life. You are always processing information, articles, or blogs you read through the filter of the story on which you are working. You are going to be inundated with lots of ideas. Sometimes when you are working on a story, you might start thinking about a new story. Rather than lose that idea, or pursue it at a time like this, write it down. You're going to have to be married to your main idea. Other ideas are going to flirt with you and want you to take them home. But they might leave you in the morning. Take down the number of that other idea and call it when you're done.

Where do you put all these other seductive ideas?

My first job was as a writer's assistant for a screenwriter, Andy Breckman, who refused to fly to Los Angeles. He would not leave his office in New Jersey. He hated flying. And here's the good part — he was (and is) such a great writer that the executives came to see him. I was lucky enough to become his assistant. When I first went to work for Andy he introduced me to THE WELL.

Andy was always writing. If he was reading a book and had an idea for a scene, he would jot it down on a scrap of people. If he thought of a great joke or overheard a great line of dialogue, he would jot it down. By the end of each day, he had these little scraps of paper in his pocket. He would transfer them to a file on his computer called THE WELL.

YOU NEED TO START A WELL
Each time you get an idea for a movie, a scene, a character name, a joke, a line of dialogue, put it into THE WELL. It becomes your best resource. When writing your script, if stuck on a scene — go to the well. See what's in there. What can you use?

● EXERCISE: THE POSTER

I was driving down Wilshire Boulevard a few years back, heading toward home; it was the magic hour. Stuck in the traffic that is Los Angeles, I looked up at some men unfurling a large movie poster. A huge billboard-sized poster. As they unrolled the poster, I began to recognize it. I recognized MY NAME. The poster was for *A Cinderella Story,* on which I was one of many producers. It was a magical moment that I couldn't write any better. I saw my name on a movie poster on a billboard.

A few months later, I was driving by when my name was being covered over. That's show business.

When you are writing your screenplay, you are the writer, the producer, the director, the star. You are marketing.

So let's market your movie. Thanks to scanners and Google Images and Photoshop, it should be easy... and fun!

I want you to do the following: Make a movie poster of your screenplay. Use any word processing program you like; if you have skills with photo editing, do that. If you like to physically cut and paste, get some scissors. Use Internet search engines to find images.

I always use this exercise in my writing classes. I want my students to be able to sell me what they are going to write. Even if they don't have any artistic skills, the results are always amazing.

The poster should be on one page and should include:

- Images of your dream cast. Why not? You're writing this for actors. You should be writing it with a certain type in mind. Handsome villain. Nebbish leading man. Fun-loving blonde.
- What's the tagline of your movie?
- Put on your producer's hat. How would you sell this movie?
- What images can you use?

It comes back to tone. We know by looking at a movie poster what we are getting ourselves into. Do the same. Have fun.

When you are done with the poster, show it to some friends and then stick it up on the wall; or make it the wallpaper on your computer desktop. Let the poster INSPIRE YOU.

PART TWO

PLOT VS. CHARACTER: WHO WILL WIN?

CHAPTER THREE

COMEDIC CHARACTERS

THE IMPORTANCE OF CHARACTER

You need a great logline for the story to work.

You need a great character for the story to *really work*.

You need a great logline to get an executive, agent, or producer to read your script.

You need a great character for an actor or actress to sign on to that script and actually to get the movie made.

Think of the plot/logline as a fancy race car.

Unless you have someone really good behind the wheel of the car, you are going to lose the race. However, since this is a comedy, the car will crash. Let's figure out who is behind the wheel.

Who is in the driver's seat? Chances are it's some kind of fool.

Comedy is inherently the fool's journey.

A FOOL'S JOURNEY

Who is the fool? In Shakespeare's time, the fool was covertly the smartest guy on the stage. He was there to be laughed at, but he also had insight. The fool in your story is your protagonist. We will go into more specifics of what type of person he or she is in a few pages. Really there are only two in a comedy. You are either going to be creating a character who is a fool on the inside OR a fool on the outside.

THE FOOL ON THE INSIDE

The protagonist on the comic journey has something to learn. The fool might be someone like Jerry Maguire in the movie of the same name. Jerry doesn't seem like a fool. He is Tom Cruise at his best. He is a sharply dressed, very successful sports agent with a great job and a really naked girlfriend. Lots of people wish they were that foolish. His problem is on the inside. Deep down, Jerry is terrible at love. He does not know how to connect with people. He doesn't know how to love.

In *Meet the Parents,* Greg Focker (Ben Stiller) is a successful male nurse who feels a deep need to impress his future father-in-law. Everything that can go wrong, does go wrong. His actions become more outwardly foolish (Spray painting a cat?! Talk about inappropriate behavior!) as the story progresses and he continues to embarrass himself and dig a deeper hole.

But when the movie opened, he wasn't an apparent fool. He was not the fool on the outside.

THE FOOL ON THE OUTSIDE

When we first meet Ben Stone (Seth Rogan) in *Knocked Up,* he is acting like a fool. He is smoking pot in a scuba mask, boxing with boxing gloves that are on fire, sitting around with his friends categorizing when an actress appears naked on the screen. He has no job and subsists on some settlement from a car accident that may even have been a scam. This guy is a fool on the outside. It's apparent what his problem is.

Steve Martin began his career playing a fool. He carried his stand-up persona to the big screen in the movie *The Jerk,* in which he played, well, a jerk.

Steve Martin would go on to reprise the greatest fool of all comedy cinema when he carried the badge of the famous Inspector Clouseau of the *Pink Panther* movies. Inspector Clouseau originated on the stage and was brought to the screen in 1964 in the movie *A Shot in the Dark* (co-written by director Blake Edwards and William Peter Blatty, who would later go on to write the horror classic *The Exorcist*). Clouseau, as played by Peter Sellers, was a bumbling detective who seemed to always cause more harm than good. He would destroy property and drive his boss insane but always manage to get the girl and the thief.

You Gotta See

Peter Sellers played the fool on the outside to perfection in the classic *The Party.* Other Sellers movies to see include *Dr. Strangelove, Being There,* and all the *Pink Panther* movies.

Take Your Silliness Seriously

A mistake beginning screenwriters often make when writing a comedy is that they do not take their silliness seriously. Just because it's a comedy doesn't mean it has to be stupid. Good comedy is still going to have to be about something. Something dramatic. These protagonists might be fools but they are kind of just like us.

If the main character doesn't care about what is happening in his life, why should we? So whatever happens to your hero in the story needs to be the most important thing ever to him or her.

I REPEAT: WHAT IS HAPPENING IN YOUR STORY IS THE MOST IMPORTANT THING EVER TO HAPPEN TO YOUR PROTAGONIST

If there was a more interesting time in their life — then write about that! Think about it: The Delta Tau Chi Fraternity has been causing trouble on campus for years. Their exploits are legendary! But now they are placed on double secret probation, it's worse than it has ever been! The final battle with Dean Wormer has begun and our heroes, our fools, Larry and Kent, got there just in time!

What about *Wedding Crashers?* All these guys do is crash weddings. Yes, but the wedding they decide to crash is the biggest wedding they have ever tried to crash — the wedding of a U.S. Senator. It is also the wedding where they will break all of their crazy wedding crashing rules and fall in love. They will be telling this story for years.

In the film *A New Leaf,* written and directed by Elaine May, Walter Matthau plays Henry Graham, a millionaire playboy who loses all his money and has to marry rich. So he sets his sights on the nebbish and unsuspecting, shy and awkward Henrietta Lowell, played by Elaine May. He needs the money. He has to find some way to get it.

THE GIRLS CLUB

Comedy has been called a boy's club. In the current climate of the man-com, that characterization might be truer than ever. But women are patient. They are often much more patient than men. Over the history of film comedy, women have more than held their own. From the screwball comedies with Rosalind Russell going toe to toe with Cary Grant to Elle Woods taking on Harvard in *Legally Blonde*, they often win the fight.

Double threats Nancy Myers and Nora Ephron consistently deliver great comedies and put people in the seats. Nancy Meyers began her career writing with then-husband, Charles Shyer. Charles Shyer would direct their hits, which included *Private Benjamin, Baby Boom,* and the remake of *Father of the Bride.* But then Nancy began to write and direct her own material and the world laughed. Her string of hits has included directing *What Women Want,* and then writing and directing *Something's Gotta Give, The Holiday,* and *It's Complicated.*

After penning *When Harry Met Sally,* Nora Ephron rocketed to directing heights with *Michael, Sleepless in Seattle, You've Got Mail,* and recently, *Julie & Julia.*

But the first lady of directing film comedy is Elaine May. May began her career as a comedienne alongside Mike Nichols in the comedy team known as Nichols & May.

Elaine May wrote and directed *A New Leaf,* and then would direct the original version of *The Heartbreak Kid* and receive writing credit on *Heaven Can Wait.* She would work on what was regarded as one of the worst comedies ever made, *Ishtar.* An homage to the Hope and Crosby "Road" movies, *Ishtar* starred Warren Beatty and Dustin Hoffman. The film was attacked and ridiculed in the media before it even opened. *Ishtar* was a box office failure. It would be nine years before she would get another movie made. Mike Nichols (her old partner) brought her on board to Americanize the French hit *La Cage Aux Follies* in the movie *The Birdcage.*

CHARACTERS CHANGE

Your protagonist is going through a *life-changing experience* in your screenplay. The audience should get a life lesson out of that. In some ways, when they put down your script or walk out of the theater, the reader or audience has also been changed in some way.

You are aspiring for nothing less.

In all great stories, *characters change*. If they don't change, then the journey was not worth it. Comedy is inherently a fool's journey to discovery or growth. Someone is foolish or misguided in his **inappropriate goal,** goes on a journey and matures, or discovers who he really is.

I want you to start thinking about a concept developed by Lajos Egris in his book, *The Art of Dramatic Writing*: the *pole-to-pole transformation.*

Imagine a magnet. One side is positive; the other side is negative. Opposites.

Imagine the North Pole and the South Pole. There are a lot of miles between those two places. Your main character, your protagonist is going to travel a great distance during the course of the story. This journey might be emotional. The emotional journey is what is referred to as the *character arc.*

So how do you start building a great comedic character?

Since this is a book on writing comedy, you want to do it ass-backwards. Well, just backwards.

Imagine who your main character is at the *end* of the movie. Don't worry about how he or she got there. Don't worry about specifics. That's what we're going to do next. But start getting an image in your mind about where you see him or her at the end. Is he married? Has she won the big game? Is he now running a major corporation? Has she saved the world?

For example: Let's take a look at main characters from some comedies and who they are at the *end of the movie*:

- In *The 40-Year-Old Virgin*, Andy dances around in post-wedding night glow. He is happy. He has a wife. A future step-daughter.
- In *Knocked Up*, Ben Stone has a job and is in love and he's a dad. He has a new apartment. It's clean.
- In *Wedding Crashers*, Jeremy has gotten married. John gets the love of his life back.
- In *There's Something About Mary*, Ted and Mary are together.
- In *Jerry Maguire,* Jerry is in the park with his new family.

Notice how the words love and marriage slipped their way in there. It happens a lot in comedies. It happens in life, too.

It's what the fool is lacking. Shakespeare comedies almost always end in marriage and a celebration. However, *Four Weddings and a Funeral* ends with one of the most non-romantic nonmarriage proposals. *The Graduate* ends with a wedding, but then the bride runs out with the real love of her life. Love is a major component of comedies. It's something to which most audience members, readers, and even agents can relate.

We just saw who five comedic blockbuster characters were at the end of their movies. Now let's talk a look at who they were at the beginning of the movies.

- In *The 40-Year-Old Virgin*, Andy lives alone. He cannot get laid to save his life. He has all but given up. He collects action figures that he never takes out of the plastic casing. (How symbolically perfect is that?)
- In *Knocked Up*, Ben Stone doesn't have a job; he smokes pot a lot. Basically he is very irresponsible.
- In *Wedding Crashers,* Jeremy and John are hitting on anything that moves and will lie to get any girl into bed.
- In *There's Something About Mary,* Ted is a loser. He is in love with Mary but she seems unobtainable. He manages to get a date with her to the prom and gets his dick caught in a zipper.
- In *Jerry Maguire,* Jerry is a shark in a suit. An agent without a soul. He is not in a real relationship. He knows something is wrong in his life but he doesn't know how to fix it.

That's right, they were almost the opposite.

All these characters have changed. They have undergone a pole-to-pole transformation. It helps to know who they are at the end, so you can figure out who they need to be at the beginning.

In *Groundhog Day,* Phil is self-centered. He is ego-driven. At the end, Phil is helping people and living his life. In *Finding Nemo,* Marlin is an over-protective father. Worried about his son. At the end, he learns to let go.

You see how it works — the misguided FOOL has learned something and grown into maturity.

THE ROCK AND ROLL SCHOOL OF SCREENWRITING

Two of the best screenwriting instructors in the world never wrote a screenplay. They never even talked about writing a screenplay. They are rock-and-roll legends Mick Jagger of the Rolling Stones and Ringo Starr of the Beatles.

What do these two guys have to do with screenwriting and, particularly, with character?

In one of the most famous Rolling Stone songs of all time, Mick Jagger sings, "You can't always get what you want/ But if you try sometimes well you just might find / You get what you need."

Your comedic character is going to think he wants one thing but winds up with something he or she really needs. For example, in *The 40-Year-Old Virgin,* Andy wants to get laid. He enlists the help of his crazy friends. Funny stuff happens. But when he meets Trish, he falls in love with her — and he realizes that what he needs, and what he really wants, is love.

In *Forgetting Sarah Marshall,* Peter cannot get over Sarah. He wants her back. But when we first see him in the film, he is not productive. He is not writing his musical. He is a slob. By staying on vacation in Hawaii at the same hotel as Sarah, Peter thinks he can get over her or get her back. What happens? He falls in love with another girl. He then writes his *Dracula* musical. He got what he needed.

You see how it works?

The classic and must-see movie *Sullivan's Travels,* written and directed by Preston Sturges, is about Sullivan, a Hollywood director of escapist, light comedic films. The kind you want to write. Well, Sullivan wants to make a movie about the human condition: the state of man today. That movie is called *Oh Brother, Where Are Thou?* (Hello, Coen brothers!). Knowing nothing about poverty and despair, Sullivan pretends to be homeless and embarks on a journey with The Girl. Yes, that's her name in the movie. The Girl. Why? To paraphrase Sturges, "There's always a girl in the movie." At the end of the movie, he discovers love and he gets what he really needs. I refuse to tell you what happens or how it happens. Discovering *Sullivan's Travels* is one of the great joys a comedy writer can have. I will not ruin it for you.

Now back to that other rock-and-roller: Ringo Starr. He was in this little band called the Beatles. Remember them from that movie *A Hard Day's Night?* Post-breakup, Ringo and George Harrison co-wrote a song called "It Don't Come Easy," which is another main rule of screenwriting. Nothing comes easy for the main character. You want to put them through hell on this journey. Movies, and especially comedies, are about characters failing, falling down in pursuit of their goal. We want to see them get back up.

If it's easy, it's boring. And you should never be boring.

Do you really think opposites attract in real life? No way. Opposites repel each other. You want a happy, long-lasting social pairing — be involved with someone who is your clone. You don't want conflict in your love life. In the movies, opposites attract because it keeps the lovers apart. If they agreed on everything, it would be boring. We want the sparks to fly.

People can find anything to argue about. Your characters should always be disagreeing — even if they want the same thing.

REMEMBER THE FIVE "C"'s

MOVIES ARE:

CHARACTERS in

CONFLICT who make

CHOICES that lead to

CONSEQUENCES that lead to

CHANGE

SCREENWRITING SHOPPING TRIP

The following list is all you're going to need to brainstorm and break your story. Forget fancy software, most screenwriters I know still use this method; or they use some form of this on their computer.

A legal pad or a notebook
Index cards

So please, go out now and buy the following:

500 Index Cards*
Corkboard
Push Pins
Multicolor permanent markers
When you come back, turn the page.

* Yes, 500. You're a writer now. You're in this for the long haul.

PLOT VS. CHARACTER

W/hy did the chicken cross the road? Because his friends egged him on. My older daughter wrote that joke when she was seven. She got it published in the *Los Angeles Times*. I was envious of her credit.

The chicken and the egg argument of what came first is like time travel. It's a paradox.

So what comes first: plot or character? I maintain that it's always about the character. That's what is the most interesting part. Now, like most writers, I don't practice what I preach, as I learned when I handed my agent what I thought was a cool spec script — a sci-fi action comedy. He asked what the kernel was for the idea. I didn't have an answer. I thought it would be cool. The most success I have had has always been based on scripts that came out of characters.

It's easier to write a character-based script. Not easy, but, I think, easier. Once you know what your character wants, you can create obstacles. We go to movies, we read books to learn. We want to see characters making the choices we never can — or would never want to. *Sophie's Choice* anyone? Now, back to the funny...

CHARACTERS ARE ALL ABOUT MAKING CHOICES

It is always important to put yourself in the audience's seat. If you don't want to see this hero go on a journey, why would millions of paying moviegoers? Because that is what you are writing for — millions of people. A lot of pressure. But you are now a myth-maker. You are telling a story about the human condition.

And that all starts with character.

BUILDING THE COMIC CHARACTER

In every class I teach and for every project I work on, I do a version of this character worksheet. It allows me to discover who my comedic hero is. This work is never handed in to anyone. It is a worksheet for the writer.

Think of it as a brainstorming exercise. So get your stack of index cards and a marker. As you work through the worksheet (on your legal pad or on your laptop), ideas are going to pop into your head.

Just jot them down. One idea per card.

For example, when thinking about the protagonist's special talent, you might say, "She's a great tennis player!" You might think: Hmm, what if my couple plays tennis later? Write it down on a blank index card. Not in detail. Just enough for you to remember it. It should be as simple as this:

```
┌─────────────────────────────────┐
│                                 │
│     JILL PLAYS TENNIS –         │
│         SHE SUCKS               │
│                                 │
└─────────────────────────────────┘
```

Throw the index card in a pile. You'll use them later when we start building the script. Right now, we are building the character.

The main focus of this brainstorming exercise is to know who your protagonist is AT THE BEGINNING of your movie. Comedic characters change over the course of the movie. Change will usually kick in about half-way through but the full transformation is not going to be until the end.

So for most of the movie, your hero is going to be who she is when we first meet her. In fact, for most of the movie she is fighting change. No one WANTS to change. Characters tend to want things to return to normal. The way things were when the movie began.

It's only at the end that they really commit to change. Harry in *When Harry Met Sally* spends ninety minutes of the movie refusing to change. Then — finally change kicks in.

Don't worry about plot. Plot will come from character. Plot will come as we talk about comedic structure. For example, you wrote down JILL PLAYS TENNIS — SHE SUCKS.

Later, you might decide that Jill has to play her boss in a tennis championship. So you throw another card on the table.

```
┌─────────────────────────────────┐
│                                 │
│     JILL PLAYS TENNIS –         │
│         SHE WINS                │
│       CHAMPIONSHIP              │
│                                 │
└─────────────────────────────────┘
```

So now you have two scenes in you movie.

Knowing who your protagonist is will generate scenes.

For now, let's discover a little more about your leads. Well, he's Jack Black or Ben Stiller. Maybe one day if you're lucky, one of those guys will read your script and agree to be in it. If they do it's because they **loved the character** they are going to play.

They found something interesting and new that they had not played before.

Okay, let's build the comic character.

● EXERCISE: THE COMEDIC CHARACTER WORKSHEET

CHARACTER'S NAME

I love names. I spend a long time looking at names. I have one rule: NO MORE JACKS. Unless you're doing *Jack and the Beanstalk* or a movie about a Jack-in-the-box, Jack has become overused. See if you can find a name that either sums up the main character or has a distinctive sound.

One of my favorite names from a screenplay is Felix Ungar in Neil Simon's classic *The Odd Couple*. Felix is a very clean man who happens to get on everyone's nerves. Even the name Ungar is irritating. The name also sets up one of the best jokes in the movie. Oscar, Felix's sloppy roommate, returns to the apartment and is greeted with a note from Felix. The note says something about meatloaf and then ends with the initials F.U. Oscar realizes later F.U. means Felix Ungar.

In *Jerry Maguire*, Jerry's enemy is the other agent played by Jay Mohr. The antagonistic agent is named Bob Sugar. That sure sounds like a sweet talking guy. But his initials are also "B.S."

In *Knocked Up*, the fool played by Seth Rogan is named Ben Stone. When we first see him on screen, he is getting stoned.

CHARACTER'S SEX AND AGE

Sex matters. Does your character have to be a man? A woman? Why? What about age? The age of your characters is very important. Think about the reference it creates. Someone born in the 1970s has a whole different set of musical tastes than someone born in the 1990s.

For most characters, you don't have to be specific. Young twenties. Early forties. Pushing sixty will suffice. But for younger characters, it's very important. A six-year-old acts differently than a ten-year-old. A twelve-year-old is much different than a fifteen-year-old.

WHAT DO THEY LOOK LIKE?

Never forget you are writing for actors and stars. And, if you're lucky, both. So when you describe your characters, never write "She looks like a sexy Reese Witherspoon." First, you have alienated every actress other than Reese. And, if you think about it, you've kind of insulted Reese. Reese doesn't want to play Reese. She wants to play a character.

Briefly describe the character's appearance. How would someone on the street describe him? Look for a description that sums up his character.

A total slacker who hasn't pressed his shirt in years.

A walking magazine cover.

She's so good looking she could stop a gay parade.

What is their general health? Any scars? Try not to say beautiful and smart: Say she could win the Miss America contest but morally would never put on that swimsuit. By the way, actors know they are beautiful.

Scars and tattoos are always fun in movies. They also make for great stories in real life. Harry Potter's got the scar. Ronny in *Moonstruck* doesn't have a hand. In *Working Girl,* a discussion takes place about the scar on Harrison Ford's chin. In *The Proposal,* the tattoo on Margaret's back is first glimpsed and then discussed. It has a story that Margaret shares with Andrew.

The most famous scar scene in movies is from *Jaws.* Two guys sit around the table on the boat and compare scars. Kevin Smith's comedy *Chasing Amy* has an homage to the scene. By the way, the *Jaws* scene ends with a fabulous monologue by Quint as he tells the story of his... tattoo.

WHICH SIDE OF THE TRACKS ARE THEY FROM?

When the story opens is your comedic hero rich or poor? Are they going through a hard time or are they just plain lazy? (See Ben Stone in *Knocked Up).* This question helps establish what is at stake for the character. What is at stake is one of those questions development executives love to ask because it's a great question.

What does the comedic hero have to lose? In *Jerry Maguire,* when we first meet Jerry he is at the top of his game. He is first class all the way. There's a lot to lose... and he does.

In *Tootsie,* Michael Dorsey needs money to put on a play. He needs a job. He is in danger of losing his career, of not being able to work.

COOL JOB

What does he or she do? This is the fun part of the writing. Either write about a world you know really well and no one else does or DO THE RESEARCH. Research is a blast. The research is the fun part. My wife and I wrote a script called *Beer Boy.* We talked to brewmasters, and read books, but the best researching was just sitting around drinking beer. No, seriously, the best research was visiting a working brewery. It inspired us. We thought of scenes. We wrote down notes on our cards.

James L. Brooks spent years researching *Broadcast News.* He is very deliberate with his research. One of the most famous and iconic lines of film comedy is from *Jerry Maguire* when Rod Tidwell (Cuba Gooding Jr.) tells Jerry (Tom Cruise) "Show me the money!" Show me the money! Show me the money! What a great line. Cameron Crowe did not write the great line, "Show me the money." He wrote it down. He overheard it from a professional football player when he was researching before he wrote the screenplay. During research you will get scenes and dialogue.

Andy in *The 40-Year-Old Virgin* is in the service business at an electronics store and the man is not "servicing" anyone. Thematic!

WHERE DID THEY GO TO SKOOL?

Does *Rocky* work if Rocky went to Dartmouth College? Maybe, but it's a very different movie. So much for the whole loser motif. Michael Corleone of the *Godfather* did go to Dartmouth. It makes a difference dramatically when he throws away that education for the family business.

There's Something About Mary spends its first sequence in high school with Ted in love with Mary and the infamous zipper scene. *Revenge of the Nerds* is about the social rivalries in college — as is *Animal House.*

Schools are great locations.

WHERE ARE THEY LIVING?

Andy in *The 40-Year-Old Virgin* lives by himself in an apartment where a lot of items are untouched (kind of like Andy). In *The Break Up*, Gary and Brooke share a pretty nice condo in Chicago. When they break up, they try to co-exist. In *War of the Roses*, the Roses share a pretty nice house in Washington D.C. When they break up, they try to co-exist.

If you're thinking, hey, those movies sound the same. They were. Kind of. But it's the characters that make them different. That's why what you are doing now with the comedic character worksheet is so important. Now keep going...

How's Your Love Life?

We talked about how often characters fall in love during the movie — so it's important to know at the beginning: How is their love life?

In *Moonstruck*, Loretta (Cher) doesn't have much of a love life. She is getting married but she is more of a mother to the man to whom she is engaged. There is no passion. Ronny (Nick Cage), her fiancé's brother, is passionate but he too does not have a love life. In *Date Night*, Phil (Steve Carell) and Claire's (Tina Fey) marriage lacks passion.

In *Jerry Maguire*, Jerry is getting married. But is he in love? Great question. We see Jerry in the throes of passion with Avery (Kelly Preston). Their conversation is intimate and sexual but it seems superficial. And that is the point.

In *Bull Durham*, each baseball season, Annie has a fling with a new player. Nothing more. It never continues past that season. She is confusing sex and love. This situation is one of the more common confusions in comedies. And in life.

What is your character's sex life like? You need to know depending on the story you are writing. In *Wedding Crashers*, we see John (Owen Wilson) having a great sex life until someone asks him how full of shit he really is. In *American Pie*, the boys are all virgins and obsessed with losing their virginity. In *Superbad*, their goal is driven by their desire to score with some girls.

It's amazing the motivation a good sex drive will provide. Hey, wasn't that the title of a low budget movie (*Sex Drive*), which was a takeoff on *The Sure Thing,* which was a then-modern day version of the original comedy blockbuster *It Happened One Night?*

WHAT ARE YOUR RELIGIOUS BELIEFS?

It's important if it matters to the story. If you are writing a satire like *Citizen Ruth,* religious opinions and beliefs are very important.

In *Bruce Almighty,* Bruce (Jim Carrey) is angry at God. He thinks he can do a better job. If he were already a believer at the beginning of the story, then there would be no story.

RACE AND NATIONALITY

Most movies are color-blind. But if you're writing a story of a young man who married into a conservative ethnic family then ethnicity is very important. (See: *My Big Fat Greek Wedding, Fools Rush In*).

Race is very important in a movie like the classic comedy *Guess Who's Coming to Dinner.* A few years ago this was remade as *Guess Who.*

WHO DID YOU VOTE FOR?

It's actually none of my business... unless you are writing a political satire or a movie about politics. In *Dave,* Dave is seemingly a liberal who replaces a staunch conservative in the White House. Of course, he begins to change and influence policy.

In *The American President,* politics and romance collide as the President (Michael Douglas) begins dating an environmental lobbyist, Sydney Ellen Wade (Annette Bening).

GOT A HOBBY?

Characters tend to be good at something other than their profession in the story. That is, they have a hobby. Andy in *The 40-Year-Old Virgin* paints little figurines. He also collects toys and keeps them unopened in their boxes. (Theme alert).

A QUICK WORD ABOUT **THEME.**

You should have an idea of what you are writing about. Love, redemption, growing up. But theme can be like a choke collar on a dog. It can restrain you. How do you see the world? Write about that. During a lunch meeting, Rob Reiner was amazed to learn from Nora Ephron how women really felt about men and how they felt about sex and love. A movie was born. Theme is often discovered at the end of a pencil, or in this case, at the bottom of an ink jet cartridge. Have an idea of what you want to say. As you write and rewrite your script, one of your characters is going to tell you what you're really writing about.

A simple solution is to have the characters do what you love to do. We all have hobbies and passions. Give one of them to your protagonist. Put yourself in the screenplay.

Nora Ephron's characters love talking about food because Nora loves food. She was once a food critic. She is an avid cook.

Paul Rudd's character in *Knocked Up* loves fantasy baseball because writer Judd Apatow found out that Paul Rudd loves fantasy baseball.

Movie characters tend to be the best at what they do. We're writing for actors here. In *Wedding Crashers,* the guys are the best liars they can be. They can invent stories in a nanosecond. Bruce in *Bruce Almighty* is good at making people laugh. In *Up in the Air,* George Clooney plays Ryan Bingham, a man whose job it is to fire other people. He is very good at his job.

They tend to be the best because I think it appeals to the star's ego. In *The Hangover,* Alan (Zach Galifianakis) tends to be only good at messing things up: the rooftop speech, the drugs. Until they need him to win at cards, then he is really good at something!

WHAT I REALLY WANT TO DO IS DIRECT

What does your comedic hero really want out of life? Sometimes a character will want nothing. This might be in a slacker comedy. In *Tootsie,* Michael wants to be a great actor. He wants to put on his friend's play. In *Superbad*, Seth and Evan are best friends going off to college. There is a party happening that night. They WANT to buy beer so they can get laid.

Do not be afraid to express what the characters want. Do not be afraid to let them wear their hearts on their sleeves. In *The Wizard of Oz,* Dorothy sings about what she wants over that rainbow.

Try it. Take a card. Write down what your character wants. You wrote down: They want to get laid. Congratulations. You probably just won over more than half the audience.

If you can keep the desire at a primal level, you are going to create empathy. You want audiences to relate to some core element of your protagonist. If your protagonist is searching for love, we get that. We can relate. If they are trying to keep their job, that's happened to most of us. Love. Hate. Revenge. Survival. Boil that need down to its essence. Does it tap into something to which everyone on the planet can relate?

"You Know What Your Problem Is..."

Early on in a movie one character might turn to the lead protagonist and say something along the lines of "Do you know what your problem is?" Yes, that character does care about his or her friend — but she or he also really cares about the audience. By asking that question, the character opens a window and we get to see what the protagonist is thinking. What are the protagonist's frustrations? What are his chief disappointments in life? What is not going right at this time? Why can't he hold a job? Why can't she fall in love?

In *Broadcast News,* Jane Craig (Holly Hunter) is a network news producer who hates the way the news is being dumbed down. It drives her mad. She is giving a speech about how she feels. We learn about it early so when she falls in love with the dumb broadcaster we're laughing.

How Do They Feel About Life?

Does your character go through life like a victim? Is he or she a negative force? A positive force? Are they lost in their own world? Do they not have a clue? Characters tend to be liars. The person they are lying to the most are themselves. They think they are happy. Chances are they're not.

Or maybe they are arrogantly happy. Fletcher (Jim Carrey) in *Liar, Liar* is a lawyer who does not care how much he lies to get what he wants. And all he wants is to be made partner.

Make Them Quirky

What are your protagonist's complexities? Obsessions? Inhibitions? Superstitions? Phobias? In *When Harry Met Sally*, Sally orders food in a very specific way. She mails letters in a very specific way. It makes her real. Harry reads the last page of every book. He wants to know the ending.

In *Annie Hall*, Alvy refuses to walk into a movie after it has started. I get this guy. I relate to him. By providing specific peculiarities, you can make your character more real. Again, put yourself in the movie. What do you like to do? This question comes up a lot. Everyone remembers Indiana Jones and his fear of snakes. It humanized a "super-hero" type of character.

Live Wire or Wallflower?

Is your protagonist the life of the party or wallpaper? Make a choice. It gives you someplace to go. In *The Hangover*, Stu Price (Ed Helms) is a wallflower who is picked on by his girlfriend who cheats on him. Alan Garner (Zach Galifianakis) is a little more of a live wire. You don't know what the guy is going to say.

WHEN I WAS A KID...

What were their childhood dreams? What are their memories? Sometimes we might see them as in *Splash*, when the young Alan falls into the water at Cape Cod and sees a mermaid. He's thought about it ever since.

NOW WHAT DO THEY DAYDREAM ABOUT?

What do they dream about now? Jerry Maguire thinks he is going to get married and his life is going to be great, but something goes wrong. All Michael Dorsey wanted to do was be in *The Iceman Cometh* on Broadway. It didn't work out.

ATTRIBUTES

Imagine you're filling out a dating profile or an application for a new job. There are listings for: Strength? Virtue? Faults? Weaknesses? Do the same thing for your main character.

In the original *Arthur*, Arthur's (Dudley Moore) strength is his friendship with his butler, Hobson (John Gielgud). Arthur's weakness is he is a drunk. He is worried about losing close to a billion dollars.

In *Tootsie*, Michael Dorsey is too opinionated. The opening montage of the movie is a primer on setting up the character's attributes. By the time the credits are over we see that Michael is a very good actor and acting teacher; he can play any part; he is passionate about what he does. But we also see that he is difficult to work with and is always getting fired

IS THERE A GHOST IN THERE?

Is your protagonist haunted by an event from his past? Are they a little screwed up in the beginning? They might be. Why? What caused this? Why is Margaret (Sandra Bullock) in *The Proposal* so alone when we meet her? We'll find out later.

Sometimes we see what causes characters to be the way they are. That ghost that caused them pain is still with them. In *There's Something About Mary*, Ted's ghost is a zipper. His memory of what happened on prom night has him in a therapist's office. In *Moonstruck,* Loretta (Cher) believes she is cursed and has bad luck. Her husband died years ago. She meets Ronny (Nick Cage), who blames his brother for how he lost his hand. Sometimes a character's past becomes the present and determines the future.

WHAT IS THEIR MAIN PROBLEM?

We're going to be developing this issue at length in the next chapter. But think about the external problem — the main problem that will drive the story. This problem determines the objective/desire/dramatic need. What do they need to do? This objective/desire/dramatic need will become the inappropriate goal. In *Knocked Up,* Ben (Seth Rogen) gets Alison (Katherine Heigel) pregnant. That is their problem.

In both versions of *The Heartbreak Kid,* the newly married husband realizes he married the wrong woman and falls in love with someone else — on his honeymoon! Talk about an inappropriate goal!

WHAT DO THEY REALLY WANT IN LIFE?

What drives your character? What is their passion? What do they care most about in the world? Again, by the end of the movie, this passion will change. But when we first meet them, it is the most important thing in the world. Often it will have to do with a career. Bruce in *Bruce Almighty* wants to be taken seriously as a news journalist. Even the Ghostbusters in *Ghostbusters* want their work to be taken seriously.

COMIC VISION

I suggest you rent two musicals and watch two numbers that sum up comedy. The first is "Make Em Laugh" from *Singing In the Rain.* The second is by Sondheim. Who would have "thunk" that the great Stephen Sondheim nailed what comedy is with his opening song to *A Funny Thing Happened On the*

Way to the Forum. If you don't know, listen to it now. A tragedy tomorrow! A comedy tonight! Comedy and tragedy are close cousins. It's all about *comedic vision.* How we see the world.

Comedic characters tend to see the world a little differently. They see the faults and the odd moments that make us laugh. You should see it that way too.

There is Woody Allen's New York and Martin Scorcese's New York: two completely different worlds. You need to live in Woody's. So should your characters. It's funnier, cleaner, and you won't get shot and stuffed in the back of a trunk.

INAPPROPRIATE BEHAVIOR

If the goal is not inappropriate, then the behavior is — or the choices the character is making might be. Sometimes it's for the right reasons.

In *True Lies*, Secret Agent Harry Tasker (Arnold Schwarzenegger) thinks his wife Helen Tasker (Jamie Lee Curtis) is cheating on him and he proceeds to use all his professional abilities to track down her lover. Is this appropriate behavior for a CIA agent? Of course not. Is it funny? Yes. What's even funnier is that he learns his wife wasn't even cheating on him.

In *Bull Durham* Annie (Susan Sarandon) chooses one minor league baseball player each season to be her lover. She teaches them everything she knows and then tosses them aside when the season ends. Appropriate behavior? Hardly. In *Kingpin* Woody Harrelson decides to take a bowling protégé under his wing. The only problem: The protégé is a naive Amish boy. Not an appropriate character for Woody to be introducing to the world of sex and drugs.

In a family-friendly movie like *Liar, Liar* a lawyer displays inappropriate behavior by being cursed — and having to tell the truth.

Your character is going to be displaying some sort of inappropriate behavior.

INAPPROPRIATE BEHAVIOR + INAPPROPRIATE GOAL = LAUGHS

It is almost like the argument of what comes first, the chicken or the egg. What comes first — the goal or the behavior? It depends on the comic character. But by the second act of your screenplay, you're going to want to be firing on both of those cylinders.

Old School has an inappropriate goal and inappropriate behavior as three grown men, Mitch, Frank, and Beanie (Luke Wilson, Vince Vaughn, and Will Ferrell), decide to start their own fraternity on campus. Granted they're no longer college students, two of them are married, and one even has a child. But that's not going to stop them. If they were nineteen-year old college students, starting a fraternity would be a reasonable goal. But it's not when you've got a kid in a car seat and a wife. The comedy is fueled by the sight of middle-aged and elderly (Blue) men acting like college boys.

In stoner comedies, the most common and obviously inappropriate goal is to get drugs, get stoned, or get drugs to get girls.

This is Spinal Tap revolves around an aging rock band that tries to make a comeback. It's hard enough for most bands to make a comeback. But make them older, very loud, and unable to open concerts and suddenly it's inappropriate and very funny. Add to that vision inappropriate clothing and dialogue and you've got a memorable comedy.

INAPPROPRIATE DIALOGUE

In *Knocked Up,* when Katherine Heigl's Type-A Allison character tells Seth Rogan, her one-night stand, "I'm pregnant." His response is: "Get the fuck out of here." Clearly not the right response. Comedic characters tend to say things that are not appropriate.

71

Unity of Opposites

Up until now we have been focusing on the protagonist of your screenplay. As we proceed on this page, we will discuss other characters and what their functions are in a story. One tip you need to keep in mind: *Don't make your characters alike.* It is boring. The smash hit *The Hangover* features three friends who lose the groom two days before the wedding. They are a good-looking, private school teacher who hates his life, a nebbish henpecked dentist, and a slightly off-center future brother-in-law. Their different personalities allow them to constantly clash and argue about what to do. If they are the same type of people, they will have the same voice. That's dull.

So you make them different. This idea is the Unity of Opposites. It is a theory credited to that master comedian, the pre-Socratic Greek philosopher Heraclitus. By the way, you hear the name Heraclitus and you start thinking about jokes.

Francis Veber, the great French comedy writer/director, said comedy is a cat and dog in a room together. That is the Unity of Opposites. Jack Lemmon and Walter Matthau made a lot of people laugh playing unity of opposites characters. From *The Fortune Cookie* to the *Odd Couple* to their celebrated return in *Grumpy Old Men*, these guys were always the cat and the dog. Of course it was in the script. Neil Simon's play and subsequent comedy blockbuster *The Odd Couple* is almost its own genre.

Opposites generate conflict. Think of movies like *Old School.* All of the characters are different personalities.

COMEDY CALISTHENICS

As you begin to think of your other characters, it might help to use some sort of template. For example, let's use Earth, Wind, Fire, and Water. The screenplay you are concocting has four main characters. How do you make sure they are different? The four elements are different. So model each character after a different element and change his personality. For example, you are writing a family comedy and you need to figure out the four personalities of Mom, Dad, Teenage Sister, and Teenage Brother.

EARTH is grounded. Stable. Sometimes it has cracks in it. But, for the most part, Earth is a down-to-earth character. That could be Mom.

WIND is a blowhard. Moves a lot. Always talking. Making noises. Can be soft as a breeze and terrible as a typhoon. That sounds like a teenage daughter.

FIRE is a hothead. Always losing his cool. Hello, teenage son!

WATER is very unstable. We need it to survive but we can drown in it. It can freeze up right in front of us but then evaporate. We associate it with tears. Very emotional. Hello, Dad!

You now have four very distinct characters to begin with. Now, you try. List the eight planets (Sorry, Pluto). They are all named after gods. But they are different types. Let's imagine you are creating an ensemble movie. So write down the planets and what they represent.

Mercury — small, fast
Venus — light, goddess of love
Earth — grounded, down to earth, full of life
Mars — red, angry son-of-a-gun
Jupiter — the granddaddy; the biggest in stature
Saturn — we remember the rings...
Neptune — cold, distant
Uranus — all alone out there

Now base eight characters after the planets. They are different. This will generate conflict, which will lead to comedy.

ROWING A SINKING BOAT

Here's what's happening in comedies: People have problems. They have flaws. They have situations or relationships or jobs that cause them worry and grief. They are occupied with this issue — so absorbed with it that when the story opens it is ruining their lives, BUT they don't know it… It's like they are rowing a sinking boat and they have no idea that they are not going to make it.

And then this other thing happens — this *event* — that the protagonist cannot deal with because she has to worry about rowing that sinking boat.

She is rowing a sinking boat and hits an ice-berg. But what happens is this event — this movie — *fixes* the hole in the boat.

So, like in *What Happens In Vegas*, Jack is not doing what he loves; Joy is in a bad relationship and worried about her job. Then, she and Jack get drunkenly married and win a Vegas jackpot but are stuck with each other as a married couple that does not want to be married. They wind up solving each other's problems — helping each other discover who they really are.

So ask yourself — what are the problems that need solving for the hero when the story opens? The problems they don't have time to deal with because the movie happens…

FUNNY PEOPLE

L et's start rounding out the story. Let's bring in some more funny people. We're going to need them. All we have so far is a comic logline and the making of comic characters.

Good start. You don't want your protagonist to be lonely. So let's start thinking about the *other funny people* in the script. Here is where you are being your most God-like. You are placing other characters in your story to serve your story.

You need to be pragmatic. You need these other characters to make the story work; to make it more interesting.

But here's the catch: these other characters have no idea that they're there to serve your story. You know who the protagonist is. You know what the star part is, but the other characters in the movie don't.

Every character in the story believes the story is happening to them — they think they are the hero.

And they should: It makes them real. From the sidekick to the antagonist, the character acts as if he or she were the lead. When we are done, you should be able to tell the same story from everyone's point of view. Let's look at *There's Something About Mary*.

The movie is about Ted, who hires a detective to find the girl he loved in high school, Mary. He is the protagonist. The good guy. Well, for a stalker at least. He's a fool. He needs to learn a lesson, and he will.

But the movie is also about Mary. A girl who moved down to Florida, and changed her name to get away from a stalker. She is now being wooed by three guys in her life — Healy, this guy who just moved down here with his sexy big teeth; Roger, the British handicapped architect, and Ted, that guy she liked in high school.

But the movie is also about Healy, a detective who goes down to Florida on a case and sees Mary. He is smitten. He thinks that if this Ted guy is stupid enough to let her go once, he doesn't deserve her. Healy is determined to win her.

Or, is it about Tucker, a.k.a. Norm the pizza delivery guy, who is obsessed with Mary? Everyone has a story. Everyone has a beginning, middle, and an end.

Great comedic screenplays have characters who *steal the show*. It's an old theater expression. You're watching a play and there is one character, one actor who stands out more than the other members. They steal the show. It wasn't supposed to be about them but it is.

In the movie *Superbad,* the character Fogell, who would later be called McLovin (as played by Christopher Mintz-Plasse), comes close to stealing the movie. His antics with the policemen played by Seth Rogen and Bill Hader were some of the biggest laughs in the movie. Of course, the crazy policemen came close to stealing the show, too.

In *Forgetting Sarah Marshall,* Aldus Snow (Russell Brand) steals the show for a while. So much so that he later gets his own movie *(Get Him to the Greek)*

Nothing should ever be wasted when writing a comedy, or any screenplay. If you are going to use a bit, a gag, or a small character, see if you can use them again later in the script. Kristin Wiig's one-liners as the network exec in *Knocked Up* became a great running gag. She steals the scene!

CHARACTER TYPES

Over the years certain types of characters have been popping up in comedies. I have given them categories. I hope this gives you a good jumping off point for developing your team of funny people. One of these might be your protagonist.

THE SMART GUY OR THE SMART GAL

The Smart Guy and the Smart Gal are comedic characters who think they know it all. They have a certain amount of arrogance. They tend to believe that they know what they are talking about and that you'd be wise to listen to them. But with this arrogance comes loneliness. No matter how smart they are in life, they aren't that smart with love and have a lot to learn.

Examples: Michael (Dustin Hoffman) in *Tootsie*, Hitch (Will Smith) in *Hitch.*

THE TURTLE

The Turtle is someone who keeps to himself. Very withdrawn.

Think of the Turtle as someone who needs to come out her shell. An introvert. The ghost or the backstory is what puts them in the shell. Turtles tend not to be the life of the party. They might be in a relationship but it is not as fulfilling as it should be.

Example: Peter (Paul Rudd) in *I Love You, Man,* Andy (Steve Carell) in *The 40-Year-Old Virgin.*

MAN-BOY

It's a man who acts like a boy. A grown up who shirks responsibility. Some dude who just wants to drink beer and smoke pot. He has no real desire to settle down. Why should he? Life is a party. The Man-Boy has a lot of growing up to do. He will get there. It's usually with the help of a new love.

Example: Ben Stone (Seth Rogan) in *Knocked Up,* Arthur (Dudley Moore) in *Arthur,* Will Ferrell in almost anything he does.

SNOBS

The snob or snob-tress (or Prince or Princess); the career girls or guys who are totally driven and defined by what they do. They might be in a relationship but it's the wrong relationship. They think their life is perfect but they will come to realize that something is missing in their lives. We like them for getting knocked down a few notches.

Examples: Louis Winthrope III (Dan Aykroyd) in *Trading Places,* Judy Benjamin (Goldie Hawn) in *Private Benjamin.*

OUT OF TOWNER

This character is the fish out of water. The guy or gal that doesn't fit into the environment. He or she is completely out of place but doesn't care. He or she will not try to fit in. They follow their own bliss.

Examples: Borat (Sasha Cohen) in *Borat*; Zohan (Adam Sandler) in *Don't Mess With the Zohan.*

WILD THING

The Wild Thing is the life of the party. Someone always getting you in trouble. It might be the lead who needs to settle down or it might be a sidekick character who serves as a catalyst to get the movie going. Sometimes in a comedy the wild thing is a mentor. This dynamic is not a good thing. The out-of-control guy often teams with the straight-laced guy.

Examples: Alan (Zach Galifianakis) in *The Hangover*; Betty White in *The Proposal*.

DICK/BITCH

The other side of the protagonist is The Bad Guy, the shadow. In comedies, the dark character tends to be the dick or the bitch or any other derogatory word you can think of. The Dick should represent everything that the hero is subconsciously afraid of becoming. The Dick thinks he is in the right. He has a clear point of view in acting the way he acts. The Dick wants to stop the hero from achieving his goal. In *There's Something About Mary,* Ted (Ben Stiller) wants Mary (Cameron Diaz), only to be thwarted along the way by the Dick Healy (Matt Dillon). In *Old School*, the guys want to open a frat house only to be challenged and threatened by their old rival, and Dick, Dean Pritchard (Jeremy Piven).

Other Dicks: Sack (Bradley Cooper) in *Wedding Crashers*, Walter Peck (William Atherton) in *Ghostbusters*.

WHAT ABOUT ROMANTIC COMEDIES?

In romantic comedies there might not be a bad guy. So who's the Dick? The dark character may be the love interest. Harry and Sally are each other's antagonists in *When Harry Met Sally* in the same way that Ben and Alison are each other's antagonists in *Knocked Up*.

B.F.F.s

Where would we be without that special someone with whom we can share our deepest feelings; the person who says "What the hell are you doing?" when you need it most? The Best Friend not only stands up for the hero, but she also tends to ask the questions that the audience is thinking. She might be the mentor offering advice.

Jerry Maguire has many mentors and best friends. Jerry and Rod are friends, but they are constantly butting heads. They need to learn from each other, which is why they are forever linked. Jerry is very good at business but he is bad at love; Rod is very good at love but bad at business. Together, they learn from each other.

Now, while all of the above can be men or women, I want to emphasize someone very special who appears in R-Rated comedies. A woman who needs no introduction:

THE R-RATED WOMAN

The R-Rated Woman might be the female lead in the R-Rated comedy. Sometimes she might just be the obligatory girl-friend, but she doesn't have to be. She is a modern age creation. She should be more than just the patient and under-standing bride-to-be. Today's R-Rated Woman can trace her ancestry to the days of screwball comedies — a descendant of Rosaline Russell and Carole Lombard and Kate Hepburn of the golden age of cinema. In the 1950s, these smart, sassy gals were forgotten, replaced by Doris Day. Audrey Hepburn as Holly Golightly in *Breakfast at Tiffany's* was her own lady — but for the most part, the gals were put into the kitchen.

What a waste.

Actresses tended not to want to do romantic comedies when they could go off and play more interesting roles in dra-matic works. We exempt Diane Keaton (*Annie Hall*) from this bunch. With the resurgence of the R-Rated comedy, we have seen some great comedic parts for women. I think it all started with an orgasm. Sally's (Meg Ryan) fake orgasm in Katz's deli in *When Harry Met Sally* to be exact. Harry (Billy Crystal) was always getting the upper hand; always getting the bigger laugh. And then something happened — Sally held her own. She didn't just hold her own. She totally one-upped Harry. She beat him at his own game. She owned the scene. Stole it. And, as a character, Sally was able to play with the boys. She was confident but vulnerable. She could cry, curse, and fake coming — and we loved her for all of it.

In today's comedy world, the R-Rated Woman is independent, opinionated, fierce; she has her posse of girlfriends, plays ball, smokes pot, and is not afraid to say what she wants in the bedroom.

Remember *Wedding Crashers*? Jeremy (Vince Vaughn) is talking a mile a minute. He is bullshitting gals left and right. Then he meets Gloria (Isla Fisher). He seduces her with his standard lines and has sex with her on the beach. At which point she acts like she is obsessive. She is all over him. She is giving him a rub job under the table. He wants to escape. He thinks she is psycho. He thought he was the Smart Guy and could just get away with his game of wedding crashing seduction. He is panicked. He is being taught a lesson, being beaten at his own game by the R-Rated Woman, and we discover Gloria has been playing him the whole time.

In *There's Something About Mary*, there truly is something about Mary. She loves football. She smokes pot. She plays golf. She jokes about vibrators. She takes care of her brother. The perfect gal.

Here are some of my favorite R-Rated Women from recent comedies. I suggest you watch them all for these memorable and hysterical moments:

Annie (Susan Sarandon) in *Bull Durham*. My favorite moment: when she calls out Crash's name when making love with "Nuke" (Tim Robbins) and defends herself by saying: "Honey, would you rather I were making love to him using your name, or making love to you using his name?" That is a total R-Rated Woman answer.

Michele (Alyson Hannigan) at the end of *American Pie* — when she concludes the story of what happened at band camp to the unsuspecting Jim (Jason Biggs). And, of course, everyone in *Bridesmaids*.

● EXERCISE: CHARACTER WORK

Comedy is exaggeration. So you have permission to exaggerate here. Take liberties. Make fun of your loved ones.

PART ONE — CAST YOUR FAMILY

Go through the comedy archetypes and assign one to each of your family members, or group of friends, or co-workers. Is your sister the R-Rated Woman? Is your Dad The Turtle? List them. If you want — cast them. Which actors would be great at playing your parents?

Assign them some qualities you know your friends or loved ones have.

PART TWO — THE ELEVATOR EXERCISE

No one wants to be stuck in an elevator with his or her family. They just don't. Now imagine being stuck with your family in an elevator! For two hours! Every one wants the same thing — to get out of the elevator. Why? Are they claustrophic? Do they have some place they have to be? Can they not stand being with each other?

I don't know. It's up to you. You and your family are stuck in an elevator. What happens next? The conflict is going to come out of character in this one. Who emerges as the leader? What is the plan of action?

The one rule: They can't all agree with each other. Alliances can be formed. But there needs to be disagreement.

Dig deep.

Write a three-to-five page scene of YOUR FAMILY STUCK IN AN ELEVATOR.

Comic voices should emerge.

CHAPTER FOUR

HILARITY AND HEART

Get those index cards ready. We're going to start developing the story. As you do, keep in mind: It has to be about something. There is the dramatic question — what is going to happen — and the thematic question — what is it really about?

Comedy works when there is a balance of hilarity and heart. The biggest comedy blockbusters have not been only about making people laugh. Sure, that's why they go — to laugh away their troubles for a while. But aside from farces, which are designed broadly and superficially, comedy blockbusters need to have heart. They need to have emotional thematic resonance underneath the humor. *Wedding Crashers* has some of broadest laugh-out-loud moments in a recent comic blockbuster. From the football game that almost kills Jeremy (Vince Vaughn), to the man-rape that almost traumatizes Jeremy, to the rub job under the table that almost... let's just say a lot happens to Jeremy in the movie. Big. Broad. Comedy trailer moments.

But if you look at the movie again, what is it really about? It's a story about friendship. More specifically, it's about the friendship that exists between Jeremy and John. When the movie opens they are celebrating a birthday. They are a couple. Best friends. At the end of the second act, they break up. They are no longer friends. They are apart. At the end of the movie, they reconcile.

Even *American Pie* has heart when Chris (Chris Klein) decides that love and honor is more important than telling the truth that he lost his virginity. In *The Hangover,* the wolf pack becomes one. A bond is formed.

As you develop the story, remember it's a comedy. But for the characters in the story, it's dramatic. Very dramatic. They stand to lose all. Love. Family. It might not be life or death but they stand to lose a last chance for happiness.

STRUCTURE: THE COMEDIC ROADMAP

Screenwriting is not linear. You should always be thinking about the beginning, the middle, and the end at the same time. The writing is more elliptical. When breaking your story, you are always going back and forth and adding elements.

KNOWING THE BAR

I'm not talking about the myth that writers drink. In fact, don't when you're writing. Exercise. Keep your mind alert. And, most importantly, nothing is more important than reading screenplays in the form the screenwriter has written them. A lot of screenplays have been published in book form. Check your bookstore.

If you can (and you can thanks to the magic of the Internet), you should be reading as many scripts as you can get your hands on. Preferably these are screenplays that have not yet been produced.

You want to know how high the bar is for material that is being shopped around Hollywood. You can't get that from reading the scripts of Preston Sturges (though you should read those, too).

Many web sites track the daily sales of screenplays. Find them. Read the industry trades (*Variety*, *Hollywood Reporter*, deadline.com) each day to see who has bought what script. By reading screenplays that have been sold, you get a feel of how a good script reads. Comedic screenplays are shorter than dramatic screenplays. Comedies tend to run anywhere from 95-110 pages. That's it. If an exec is reading a 122-page comedy, chances are she is not buying it. Executives talk about white on the page. That's a script that tends to be dialogue heavy and is a quick read.

BACK TO STRUCTURE

So, how does structure help? It helps any one of your sections from becoming too long or too boring. Structure can be learned. How? By watching a lot of movies. By reading scripts. As you watch and read movies and screenplays, you will begin to anticipate what will happen next.

Structure implies a strong line of dramatic action. A strong structure means you have a story that goes somewhere; a story that moves forward — beat by beat, scene by scene, comedic sequence by comedic sequence.

Structure is cause and effect. It is action and reaction. You are going to think about your structure in terms of events.

By now you have an idea of who your characters are. You have a sense of what they are doing in your story. Most importantly, you know where they are going to be at the end. So how do we make them dance? Give them a dance floor on which to work.

THE "CLASSIC" AND STILL MODERN THREE-ACT STRUCTURE

Everything has a beginning, a middle, and an end. There's Act One, Act Two, Act Three. These are terms taken from the theater. Act One implies the curtain going up. At the end of Act Three the curtain goes down. The play is over. You are writing without the curtains.

In a 120-page script Act One would be about thirty pages, Act Two about sixty pages, Act Three another thirty. There's a balance. Most books we've read repeat the same structure with minor variations.

Here is one way to simplify structure in terms of punctuation:

Act One ends with a *dramatic question*. We wonder what is going to happen. Is the protagonist going to achieve his goal?

Act Two ends with an "Oh No!" It's the "Oh No!" moment where all seems lost. We are over-simplifying here for the overview. Think exclamation point!

Act Three ends with a period. There's finality to the story. It's over.

I like to divide Act Two into two acts: Act Two-A and Act Two-B. The divide is at the *midpoint* of the story. The midpoint is treated like a curtain coming down at the intermission of a Broadway show. So, in some ways, Hollywood is working in a four-act structure. But no one will ever say that. Can Hollywood count to four? Not sure.

The midpoint is like another act break and it's also balanced. So a 120-page script's Act Two would be divided into a thirty-page Act Two-A and a thirty-page Act Two-B. Please note: Not every script is 120 pages.

As I said — comedies tend to be shorter. With a lot of white on the page.

It makes it easier to read.

Like this.

See?

Scripts might run from 100-110 pages. If that's the case, do the math. Page 55 would be the midpoint.

Can your script be longer than 120 pages? Sure. By a few. But if a comedy is longer than 120 pages, get ready to be turned down fast.

But know this: If you're a first timer, here's what might happen: Your agent will send over your script to a studio executive. The exec will turn to the back and look for the number of pages. If it's more than 120 pages, the exec will frown. Here's why: The exec is looking to see that you, the writer, have done your job. Page length suggests that the writer knows what she is doing.

All movies are mysteries. Or they should be. Not in the sense that we are following a detective solving a crime, but because we should always be wondering: *What is going to happen next?*

Screenplays should pose questions that will be answered over the course of the story. Will the boy and girl get together? Will their fathers find out?

As the plot thickens and the subplots are introduced, more questions are raised. If a screenplay asks questions, the reader will turn the page to look for answers.

● EXERCISE: QUESTION EVERYTHING

Today is going to be a busy day. I'm giving you homework. You will need some way to take notes and watch a DVD. A comedy, perhaps. I think that's a good idea, as this book is about writing comedies.

I want you to watch a movie and write down every question raised by the movie.

Just list them — anything that might spark a question in the audiences' minds. Will he get the job? Will she get the guy? For example, let's look at *The Hangover.*

What happened to the groom?

Will they get married?

What happened to the car?

Will Stu get engaged?

Whose baby is it?

What happened last night?

Why is there a tiger in the room?

Why are people trying to kill us?

Where's my tooth?

Why do we have a police car?

All of these questions (and more!) get answered. In the end credit sequence, we finally learn what happened during the night.

As you develop your story, you need to start presenting your characters with questions that the plot is going to answer.

THE COMEDIC SEQUENCE APPROACH

Over the years, film structure has stayed the same but changed. Hollywood still makes movies in the classic three-act structure. The sequence approach is still in use. I think the sequence approach is the best way for a writer to develop his story.

It's very hard to write a 112-page script. But can you write a fourteen-page script? "Sure. I can do that," you think. Well, that's what we're going to do.

We're going to write eight comic sequences, labeled A–H. Each one is going to translate into fourteen pages of screenplay. Each comic sequence will have a beginning, a middle, and an end.

Each comic sequence is different. Think of comic sequences like movements in a symphony. I have always thought of classical music as very similar to films. There are different movements, different pacing of the composition where the main theme repeats and re-emerges, carried by different sections of the orchestra, just as the themes of a movie are carried by different characters. They crescendo at the end with a rousing conclusion.

Each comic sequence has a name, giving it dramatic context.

Now, if you are going to groan that there are no rules. I'm going to say there are. There is really only one rule:

DON'T BE BORING.

Seriously, if you can keep the readers interested, you're going to succeed. You want them to turn pages.

But you need to know how to do that. The comic sequence approach is a way to keep your story moving, to keep it interesting. It is based on the "sequence" approach. The sequence approach has been around for years.

Preston Sturges, the original comedy writer/director, broke his screenplays into sequences. The screenplays for *Sullivan's Travels* and *The Lady Eve* are broken into twelve sequences.

Alfred Hitchcock used the sequence approach. See *North by Northwest.* There's the "crop duster" sequence, the "seduction on the train" sequence. The movie ends with the "fight on Lincoln's nose" sequence.

Here's what the comic sequence does differently: Each comic sequence has a very clear dramatic context. When you are writing the first comic sequence (and we'll break this later) you are only dealing with elements that have to do with that sequence: *The Comedic World.*

WRITING THE SCRIPTMENT

Treatments are boring. No one reads them. They don't reflect the tone of what you are writing. You want to write the script. But you are not ready to write a script. So let's work on a scriptment.

How does it differ? I think the scriptment elicits a more emotional response from the reader. It is not a list of this happens and that happens.

I always tell my students when they are pitching, or writing the scriptment: Imagine you're telling the story to a ten-year-old, not because most executives act like ten-year-olds but because I find that the writer is impatient and will gloss over key plot points, or rush things and create huge gaping holes of logic that can never be filled.

We want to work out all the problems in the story now, *before* you begin to write.

After each chapter, an assignment corresponds to what you have read. Do it. This scriptment phase is for you to develop and craft your movie.

It is writing.

So let's get writing...

SCENE STUDY

The scriptment is made up of eight comedic sequences. Within those sequences are usually *five events*. Within those events are *scenes*. We're going to be carding out your story as you progress. When you're finished, you will have forty index cards. Each one will have an *event* on it. Events are a series of scenes strung together around the same context. So there might be two cards in a sequence that read like this:

ALLIE STEALS A CAR

**ALLIE CHASED BY
POLICE – ESCAPES
THROUGH CHINATOWN**

Before you would be able to write those events, you will need to know what is inside of the events. Inside are scenes.

When I first started teaching, I would talk about structure and then scenes at the end. The problem I found was that it's impossible to build a bowl unless you know what you are going to put in it.

Structure is the bowl.

Events and scenes are what go in the bowl.

Scenes are continuous action within the same time and place; they can last anywhere from one line to five pages. Scenes vary in pacing. They should. They should not all have the same rhythm.

When you write a scene, it might be like this...

```
INT. OFFICE — DAY

Keith sits at his desk. Laughs.
```

We know we are inside because of the INT. (which stands for Interior). We know where we are — my office. We know it is day. The above is not a good scene. Why? Nothing happens.

Remember the don't-be-boring part.

Scenes and events are made up of actions and verbs. Think of your story in terms of actions and verbs and things happening and you will be fine.

Something needs to happen. These are the events in the story. Structure is setting up the character, having events happen, and then having the character react to those events.

WHAT MAKES A SCENE GOOD?

How does a scene work? What causes a script to slow down so much that the reader wants to put it down? Chances are the scene work is bad. Chances are the reader is reading a scene that should not be in the movie. How do you know if a scene belongs? Scenes should:

- Move the story forward
- Provide character insight
- Or, provide information to the audience

How do we craft scenes? Let's say you have an idea for a scene. The first thing you should do is:

DEFINE THE DESIRE

Movies might be described as this: *Somebody wants something and is having trouble getting it.* Scenes are basically the same. While there are overall objectives for a screenplay (that is, the protagonist has a main goal) each scene has a smaller goal — but something just as important to the hero. This is called *writing in the moment.* The protagonist is only concerned with the *objective of the scene.* What does the protagonist need to gain in that scene? At this moment in the story, what do they need most? We talked about living in the moment with these characters. This is what we need to do. Who wants what? Who is driving the scene?

I sketched out earlier that ALLIE STEALS A CAR. Let's say she needs that car to get to her mother's wedding to stop it before she marries the man to whom Allie was once engaged.

So her goal for the movie: The inappropriate goal is to stop the wedding. That is what she ultimately wants to do. But right now, at this moment in time she wants to steal a car. She's compelled to do so. It's the only way she can get to the wedding.

So the desire in the moment is to STEAL THE CAR. Provide the characters with ACTION VERBS. Have them want something

To persuade.

To defend.

To seduce.

Many times on the set while shooting a movie an actor will be befuddled with a director. She is not sure what is going on. The director might talk about theme and backstory. The actor gets more confused. It's not the director's fault. It's not the actor's. It's the writer's. The script is probably underwritten — meaning, they don't know what the *want* is in the scene because the writer did not put it there.

When thinking about what scene belongs in your story, think about which character is driving the scene. Notice, I said *who is driving the scene*. It is not always the protagonist. Take a scene like one in the classic James Bond film *Goldfinger.* Goldfinger has Bond strapped to the table. He is going to kill him with a laser. He wants to torture him. He wants to kill him. It is Goldfinger's scene. Bond is lying on the table. He wants to stop Goldfinger from achieving his goal. But when you're strapped to a table with a laser burning hot between your legs, it's hard to drive the scene.

Goldfinger *wants to kill* Bond. That is the desire.

Now, Allie wants to steal a car.

GENERATE THE CONFLICT

Conflict is the life blood of your screenplay. There is nothing more boring than two people sitting around agreeing. You might be doing a historic piece about D-Day. Two generals want to invade France and drive the Nazis out. They want the same thing. So where's the conflict? One wants to invade on one beach. The other guy suggests a different beach. Conflict.

TWO TYPES OF CONFLICT

A lot has been written about what types of conflict there are. I think there are simply two. Either the problem is coming from within, or from outside forces. Let's go over the two here:

Internal Conflict: what the protagonist might carry around within him or her. It is what is really troubling the protagonist. Sometimes it relates to an inner wound or a ghost. For example, in a movie like *Honeymoon in Vegas*, the internal conflict in Jack Singer (Nick Cage) is that he promised his mother on her deathbed that he would never get married. As the story progresses, he has to deal with the inner conflict. Finally, at the end of the movie, he is whole.

In *Groundhog Day*, Phil is stuck living the same day over and over again: Finally when he doesn't act in a selfish manner, things go right and he wakes up. An inner conflict is sometimes referred to as *man vs. man.* Think of your protagonist as being his own worst enemy. In movies like *Liar, Liar* this conflict is born as soon as Fletcher is cursed. In *A Beautiful Mind*, the Russell Crowe character is mentally ill.

What is troubling your main character? What is making him or her unhappy and unable to have that complete life?

External Conflict: I just mentioned *Honeymoon in Vegas.* What is the external conflict? The gambler Tommy Korman (James Caan) is in love with Jack's fiancée, Betsy (Sarah Jessica Parker.) Tommy has taken Betsy to Hawaii for the weekend. Jack is determined to win her back. Tommy knows Jack is coming and does everything he can to have him stopped — from pairing him with a crazy cab driver who gets him in a hut with Chief Orman, who just wants to sing songs from *South Pacific,* to forcing Jack to take a plane and join a troupe of flying Elvises. Remember, it don't come easy.

External conflicts come from *characters and situations* that get into the protagonist's way.

Do you ever wonder why so many people have trouble starting their car at the worst possible moment? Because the writer always knows there should be conflict. Everywhere. Look at the scene you're thinking about and then try to come up with as many things as you can to throw at your character. External conflict can be weather, objects, hills to climb, doors to open, a dog to deal with, a kid with an attitude, the teacher who won't give you a good grade. *Nothing should come easy.*

Remember we had the card ALLIE STEALS A CAR. Well, what if she has to steal her own car just as it is being auctioned off at the police impound? Maybe her mother's engagement ring is in the car so she has to steal it in front of ten policemen.

Or maybe it's a not car. It's an ice cream truck. And she has to steal it from a children's party. You decide.

BREAK THE SCENE INTO BEATS

When writing a scene, I do a lot of left margin writing. I never worry about writing the text of what will happen first. I suggest you try this. Concentrate on the beats of the scene. The "beats" are the little moments that happen in the scene.

Let's think about the zipper scene from *There's Something About Mary.* If it were a card on our board we would call it:

PROM NIGHT — TED GETS
HIS JUNK CAUGHT IN
ZIPPER

What are the beats of that event?

- Ted arrives at house
- Mary's dad messes with him, says Mary's not home
- Mary comes down the stairs — Beautiful
- Ted gives Warren a baseball
- Warren beats up Ted
- Mary goes upstairs to fix dress
- Ted goes to bathroom
- Sees Mary changing
- Peeping Tom
- Ted pulls up zipper too fast!

Those are the beats. When thinking about what you're going to write, think about the beats first. The small things. You are going to write toward the *most important beat*. Make sure the scene makes sense before writing the action.

FIGURE OUT THE TURNING POINT — THE UNEXPECTED

Every scene should have a *turning point*. The turning point is like the act break of the scene. Something happens that turns the scene and leads into the next scene. It's good if it's something *unexpected* — something that surprises the protagonist and the reader. It changes the momentum of the scene. It was heading one way and then something turns it. *Always go for something unexpected.* I'm not suggesting scenes of alien spaceships landing. I am suggesting scenes that *move the story forward*.

Remember: *Scenes need to move the story forward, provide character insight, or provide new information to the audience.*

All of the above result in a turning point. The turning point of the scene does not always need to be a physical act. It can be a piece of information new to the audience or to the character. These can all be considered turning points. Audience insight counts. You want to keep the audience involved. Let them keep asking questions.

Let's look at the beats of the prom night scene in *There's Something About Mary*. If we broke it up into actual scenes, INT. and EXT. would fall in the following way:

EXT. MARY'S HOUSE — DAY

- Ted arrives at house
- Mary's dad messes with him, says Mary's not home

The unexpected in the scene and in the movie is that (1) Mary's Dad is African-American (played brilliantly by Keith David). Also, that Mary's Dad tells Ted that Mary is not home. He is joking with him and lets him inside the house. It makes a short scene funny. It has conflict.

INT. MARY'S HOUSE — DAY

- Mary comes down the stairs — Beautiful
- Ted gives Warren a baseball
- Warren beats up Ted
- Mary goes upstairs to fix dress
- Ted goes to bathroom

Above are the beats of the next scene. Notice how the scenes have a beginning, middle, and an end. Also the end of the scene *leads us to the next scene*. Scenes should spin into scenes; events should spin into events; sequences should spin into sequences; acts should spin into acts. It's dizzying!

INT. BATHROOM — DAY

- Ted sees Mary changing
- Peeping Tom
- Ted pulls up zipper too fast!

Because Warren beat up Ted, Ted finds himself in the bathroom. He looks up and sees Mary in her bra. He freaks out that Mary's Mom thinks he is a Peeping Tom. He whips up his zipper — too fast — and gets the very *unexpected* as the zipper catches his "junk" in his pants. The scene ends with a scream (from Ted and the audience) and leads us to the next event.

Later, when going through your scriptment if the scene does not do any of the three things it should do, get rid of it. It probably doesn't belong in the movie.

ADD A BUTTON

Always start your scene as late into the action as possible, and get out as soon as it's over. How do you know when it's over? When the scene has accomplished what you needed it to accomplish. When it has pushed you to another scene.

If you can, end with the funniest line or moment. Sometimes this arrangement is called adding a button to the scene.

As a general rule, don't bury your jokes. They need to come at the end of the dialogue, end of the scene description, or end of the scene.

PUTTING SCENES TO WORK IN EVENTS

When a series of scenes are strung together around the same theme/piece of action, they might be called *events*. I like to think of them as events in the movie. Here's why: A sequence always ends on a dramatic piece of information; something unexpected has happened and the author forces you to turn the page to see what happens next. Also, usually something has changed. Someone was happy in the beginning of the sequence, but at the end she is sad. We are always looking for a *change* — a change from positive to negative or vice versa. A change in the situation.

We will build these events with forty index cards.

EXERCISE: FUNNY SCENES

You can't write a movie without knowing how to write a scene, so let's do a scene exercise. Based on you life!

The most embarrassing moment of your life.

Comedy is funny because it's happening to someone else. Most of the time. For example, no one wants to be dumped while standing buck naked in a room, as in *Forgetting Sarah Marshall*. But that scene came out of writer Jason Segel's life. It was a humiliating experience that he turned into a very memorable scene.

Now it's time for that pain, humiliation, and embarrassment to happen to you.

It's time to lose your pride. Sit back and reflect on your life. Think about the moments in your life that make you cringe, blush — the moments in your life where you felt the most embarrassed.

Dig deep. Write down the ten most embarrassing things that have happened to you.

List them.

Now which one really makes you laugh? Hopefully you can laugh about it now.

Who was there? What were you trying to accomplish when you were caught in an embarrassing situation?

Structure the event as if it were a scene. So there's going to be a set-up, a turning point, and then the embarrassing moment. Now write it: in three to five pages of screenplay. As if it were a scene in the movie. Tell us what happened. Be visual. Imagine someone is going to film it tomorrow.

THE SECRET INGREDIENTS OF COMEDIC SCENES

COMEDIC DEVICES

When thinking about your screenplay, think about what comedy devices you can use. Here is a list of some comedy devices and conventions that have been repeated in comedy blockbusters.

CROSS-DRESSING

Two of the most highly regarded comedies of all time, *Some Like it Hot* and *Tootsie,* have their protagonists dressing like women. It's also used in *She's the Man.* Cross-dressing is a comedic device that was well-utilized by Shakespeare in his comedies, and was used in *Shakespeare in Love,* in which Viola dresses like a man so she can achieve her desire to be an actor at the Globe.

DECEPTION

A major component of comedy is deception. A character might decide to dress up as someone else, or pretend to be someone else. With deceit, there must come revelation — as in *There's Something about Mary,* when Ted does not tell Mary he has been stalking her and hired a detective to track her down.

RUNAWAY BRIDE

Brides running away from their weddings has been a motif of the screwball era beginning with Ellie Andrews (Claudette Colbert) leaping from her father's yacht and winding up with Peter (Clark Gable) in *It Happened One Night.* There was even a comedy hit called *Runaway Bride* with Julia Roberts.

SEX

Sex in comedies is sometimes the laughing gas to the inappropriate comedy engine. *The Graduate* is all about a young man having an affair with older women. Scenes of seduction offer much comedy. In *Clueless*, Claire (Alicia Silverstone) tries to seduce a boy whom she doesn't realize is gay. *When Harry Met Sally* has sex as a central theme.

SONG AND DANCE

Music and comedy are long-running dance partners. Only in a comedy do people break out into song. Except for *The Deerhunter* — but it was not played for laughs. The Marx Brothers sang out loud on screen to Captain Spaulding, the African Explorer, in *Animal Crackers*. The in-joke was that Captain Spaulding referred to a well-known Hollywood cocaine dealer who had been arrested a few years earlier. Recent songs in movies include Cameron Diaz crooning horribly to karaoke in *My Best Friend's Wedding*; in *500 Days of Summer*, Tom Hansen (Joseph Gordon-Levitt) has a great song-and-dance number after spending a night with Summer (Zooey Deschanel). One of the best song and dance numbers in film comedy is when the Monster (Peter Boyle) dances and sings "Putting On the Ritz" in Mel Brooks' *Young Frankenstein*.

ANIMALS

Tap into your animalistic nature. Write an animal into your movie. It's been done before! Is it a tiger, as in *Bringing up Baby* or *The Hangover*? Is it a monkey running around with Cary Grant when he discovers the fountain of youth-type formula in *Monkey Business?* It can even have people sometimes dressed as animals. See the end of *Trading Places*.

DUMB BLONDES

Blondes have gotten a bad rap on the screen but they have provided laughs. From Judy Holliday in *Born Yesterday* and Marilyn Monroe in *Some Like It Hot*, to Reese Witherspoon as Elle Woods in *Legally Blonde,* the dumb blonde is a staple of film comedy.

VIOLENCE AND PRAT FALLS

You don't get that hurt in a comedy. Someone might fall off of a building or get a fish hook caught in his mouth, but chances are he will get up to laugh another day.

SET PIECES

A set piece in a comedy film is a long-sustained sequence of physical action. Think of it like an action scene in an action movie. In the movie *It's A Mad, Mad, Mad, Mad World,* the final chase and race into the building at the end is a huge set piece. (The movie is filled with them). In *There's Something About Mary,* a set piece is when Mary's dog is given amphetamines and fights Ted.

THE COMIC RANT

Ah, the comic rant. One of the staples of great film comedy. A motif that only works if the character delivering the rant is believable. Notice I didn't say actor. Vince Vaughn is the master of the comic rant. His moments of observation in *Wedding Crashers* are priceless, and oft-imitated.

But there are movies where it just doesn't feel right, when the ranter seems like he's trying too hard. And he might be, because the character isn't real, isn't passionate, isn't fully committed to making everyone in the scene see his point of view.

There's only so much Vince can do in *Four Christmases.* The man is trying. But it's just not working. Why? Because his character has been set up as nothing more than Vince Vaughn. Watch the movie. It's not great. No spoilers there.

We also have to believe in the *comic rant.* We have to side with the person persuading us. Remember *Bull Durham?* Early on, Crash Davis shares his philosophy of life. He tells Annie his worldview, letting her, and us, know how smart he is. He's not showing off. It's what he believes. The subtext (there's always subtext) is that if you can't see that you should be with me, there's something wrong with you. We don't know much about Crash before this rant, but we know a lot about him after it.

The comic rant can come out of frustration —like the cap on an oil well blowing. It might come out of a character who is uptight, like Steve Martin as Neal in *Planes, Trains and Automobiles*. He has only one blow-up in the movie. If he acted this way all the time, we wouldn't empathize with him. The rant has to be something we can *relate to* (we have all been frustrated at rental car counters, or any counter for that matter) and it has to be *earned*. We have seen what Neal has been going through up to this point. He is just a man desperate to get home in time for Thanksgiving.

Sometimes the comic rant is just comic. Just plain laugh-out-loud funny.

In *School of Rock* the key is passion. Dewey, as played by Jack Black, is passionate about his music; about the state of rock-and-roll today. Thematically, this idea works well, as he is a posing as a teacher. Even if the kids don't understand what he is talking about, the audience does.

And, finally, it all comes back to *Network*, written by Paddy Chayefsky. It's a dark comic tale about the state of network news in 1975. This rant is one of social commentary. The scary thing is that it has all come to pass.

Again, the rant is earned. No one wants to be screamed at. But if you pull it off, look for that moment in your screenplay where the protagonist cannot take it anymore. You might learn something about your comic hero, and teach us something about the world.

CROSS TALK

Cross talk is when two characters in the scene THINK they are talking about the same thing but are actually having two different conversations. It only works if the audience is in on the joke. The protagonist/comic hero is not in on the joke. In

There's Something About Mary, Ted (Ben Stiller) has been arrested for picking up a hitch-hiker. That is why he thinks he is being interrogated. The police have found a body in Ted's car — a dead body left there by the insane hitchhiker Ted picked up and who got away. The police think Ted is a serial killer. (Ah, the stuff of comedy).

THE R-RATED COMEDY

The R-Rated Comedy is a very hot genre now. It's comedy that people are not getting for free on television. Writers and comic stars are pushing the envelope. One fool-proof way of getting an R-Rating is to have more than three F-bombs in a script. But you can have violence and still get away with PG-13. Likewise, you can have guns in a PG-13 movie, but throw in some frontal nudity, and you've got an R-Rating. Thank you, uptight Pilgrims!

Although it might not seem like it if you listen to some talk radio stations, we have come a long way from Lenny Bruce being thrown in jail for screaming "cocksucker." Yes, it happened. The R-Rated system came about after the words "screw" and "hump the hostess" hit the screens in 1966. You're thinking, that's it? We hear worse on reruns of the TV show *Friends.*

Yes, the movie was *Who's Afraid of Virginia Woolf?* based on the Edward Albee play. A few years later MGM decided to release *Blow-Up,* which contained nudity. These movies were released without the seal of approval established in the early days of Hollywood by a guy named Jack Hays. Ironically, the Hays Code came about because of violence in the movie *Scarface.* Finally, in 1968, a deal was brokered with the studios and the theater owners and a ratings system went into effect.

As these events were unfolding, George Carlin, the comedian, came up with his "Seven Words You Can't Say on Television." Have fun — watch it on You Tube. It holds up pretty well.

PART THREE

The Comedic Roadmap — The Eight Comic Sequences

CHAPTER FIVE

COMIC SEQUENCE (A)

THE COMEDIC WORLD

A.K.A. WELL BEGUN IS HALF DONE

After graduating from New York University Film School, I was lucky enough to get a job working as a writer's assistant for Andy Breckman. (The guy who wrote the incredibly funny intro to this book!)

I did a reverse commute from my apartment in Manhattan to suburban New Jersey. At that time, Andy was working out of an office on the ground floor of a house. I walked into the office and saw a pool table.

"Cool. I'll get to shoot some pool!"

"That's not for playing pool," Andy said, "That's for the index cards. It's easy to move them around on the felt."

And he was serious. I don't think we ever played a game of pool. Andy would shout out scene ideas and I would jot them down on an index card and place them on the table.

Funny scene in the corner pocket!

He would move around the cards. And a movie would appear.

When I started working in Hollywood, I noticed other writers carding out movies. It's the easiest way to see the whole movie in front of you.

Now, you don't need to go buy a pool table. But get a corkboard. A general note about using index cards: *Do not hammer them into the wall.* One, it will tick off your landlord, spouse, etc., and it's not good for your story. The cards are meant to be moved around. Maybe your story doesn't introduce the buddy until the second act, then move the card there.

What is important is to hit the dramatic events. My suggested order is based on watching, reading, and teaching.

Do try to keep the cards within the context of your column — especially the first and last one of each sequence. But other than that — write your own song.

INDEX CARD SOFTWARE

Most screenwriting software has an index card function that creates the corkboard experience. The open source program CELTX (www.celtx.com) is good, as is Final Draft 8 (www .finaldraft.com). You must be able to see the whole movie on your screen. If you can't — then stick to the corkboards. In fact, I still prefer them because the movie is always staring you right in the face when you sit down to write.

COMIC SEQUENCE (A) A.K.A. WELL BEGUN IS HALF DONE

The structure of Act One is divided into two sequences. In the first sequence, which we will be discussing in this chapter, we are setting up the comedic character. In the second sequence of Act One, we will be setting up the story. You need to establish who your movie is about before you have a movie. Remember we talked about how characters change. This means setting up who they are before they change.

SETTING UP THE COMEDIC WORLD

Movies do not get better as they go along. Books do not get better. Someone tells you a story on the way to work; you are bored. You start thinking about how you can change the conversation — but you can't. It just keeps going on.

Movies are like that. They have to be interesting, involving from page one...

When you watch a movie how long do you give it? Ten minutes, tops. We usually know within ten minutes if we are going to like a movie. That doesn't mean we are going to love it in its entirety. It might fall apart, *but it does not get better.*

Screenplays are like that.

In the reality of the movie industry especially in our day and age of informational overload, it takes a lot for a producer or a studio exec to invest two hours of time to read your script. You might say it's their job to read it. But it's not their job to like it. You have to make them like it.

Today mostly everything is submitted electronically. We are saving trees, but Hollywood is still tossing bad scripts into the trash. It just happens to be the trash folder on their computer desktop.

So how do you keep your script out of the trash folder?

We discussed earlier how a story is engaging if it keeps asking questions. Keep the reader engaged and give them a reason to turn the pages.

Well begun is half-done

The first comic sequence is called *The Comedic World*. It comprises roughly the first thirteen pages of your screenplay. In this sequence, you want to introduce the comedic world, set up the character, and then plant a clear, inappropriate goal for your character (and, just as importantly, for your audience).

So let's start setting up The Comedic World — the dramatic context for the first comic sequence. It's all you need to worry about right now.

Like everything else — the three-act structure, character arcs, scenes — there is a beginning, a middle, and an end. Every comic sequence should have a beginning, a middle, and an end.

Think of it as a short movie. You should be able to watch any sequence in the movie and it should stand on its own. The end of each sequence will lead to the next sequence.

COMIC SEQUENCE EXAMPLE:

The 40-Year-Old Virgin

(A) The Comedic World

We meet Andy. He lives by himself. He plays poker with his friends. They find out he's a virgin.

(B) The Inappropriate Goal

Andy hopes they will leave him alone and that no one will remember what he said. They do. They want to help him. He refuses, then agrees to let his friends help him lose his virginity.

(C) The Mad, Mad, Mad, Mad World

Andy goes to a bar and hits on women of the intoxicated variety. He gets a crazy ride from Nicky (Leslie Mann) home. She throws up on him.

(D) It Just Keeps Getting Worse

Andy tries speed-dating. Tries to hit on Beth (Elizabeth Banks) in the bookstore. Andy meets Trish — likes her.

(E) Love is in the Air

Andy and Trish begin dating. Andy and Trish decide not to rush things and not sleep together.

(F) What Was I Thinking?

Andy is becoming a role model. But it's getting harder. Beth really wants him. The truth comes out.

(G) Time to Grow Up

Andy can sleep with Beth. What is he going to do?

(H) The New Me

Andy wins Trish back. Gets married. Enjoys his wedding night.

● EXERCISE: COMEDY CALISTHENICS

Remember we talked about tone? That is, what other movie is it like? If you're writing a screwball comedy in the tone of *His Girl Friday,* then you should study *His Girl Friday.* It becomes a reference movie. Reverse engineer it. Dissect it. How does it work?

I asked you to purchase 500 index cards. I suggest you use them to break down some reference movies. I am going to suggest forty cards make up your movie. As we progress, see if you can break down one of your reference movies into forty cards (forty events).

Each card/event is going to have some sort of title. Some dramatic context. You want an example? Go to your DVD collection and pull a DVD off your shelf. Open the cover and look for the *Chapter Headings.* How many are there? *Shakespeare in Love* has thirty-one chapter stops. Each one has a title like "At First Sight" or "Opening Night." They inform us of what is going to happen in that chapter of the DVD.

When you're done carding out your movie, your forty cards are going to be on the wall in front of you. That is going to be the map of your movie.

> TO DO: Card out two movies that are similar in tone to your movie.

WHAT IS THE TONE OF YOUR STORY?

One of the most important things you are going to do in the first section of your screenplay is establish the tone. When you read a script, watch a movie or television show, or read a novel, you very quickly have a feeling for the tone of the story. When watching *Shrek* for the first time, you know you are quickly in the antifairy tale. In a quick montage, *Little Miss Sunshine* establishes the various characters and their quirks, letting the audience know they are in for a dramedy.

In the first minute of *The Hangover,* we know that the bachelor party went a little out control and the guys have lost the groom.

You don't want to confuse the reader with tone.

A thriller should thrill.

A comedy should make people laugh.

You don't have much time — one to two pages of screenplay pages to be exact, one to two minutes of the movie. Again, read screenplays that haven't been produced yet. Here's why: A movie has been marketed. The tone has been conveyed via the poster, the trailer, the interviews with the stars in magazines and on TV. We know going into the theater what we are going to see.

All your screenplay has is the logline and the first few pages.

Think of it like this: You see an attractive guy or girl in the gym. You want to introduce yourself. You think about what you are going to say. You only get one chance at a *first impression.* If you blow it, they are going to blow you off.

The same is true for your screenplay. After you are established, people will read you with prejudice. After one producer validates your material, other producers will read with prejudice and be predisposed to liking it.

But now, in the beginning, when you are starting out, how you start your screenplay can start or stop your career.

No pressure.

Here is what you need to do: Before even thinking about that first scene, that first image, before writing that first page, be prepared to write what *no one will read or see;* a part of the story that will *never* be filmed but is paramount to making the first thirteen pages of your screenplay work. That is the prestory.

THE PRESTORY

The *prestory* is what happens in the movie a few days/ hours before the movie opens. If you're starting with someone going to work on a Monday — what was her weekend like? Is she worried about something going on at work? Did her best friend just confess to having an affair? Is she carrying a winning lotto ticket?

You, the writer, need to know what is happening in the world of your story and your characters *before* the audience enters that world. I have seen many writers start writing and not know where they are going. They spend ten to twenty pages figuring out the story. They muddle through scenes.

You need to know what is going on when the curtain rises. If you don't, who does? The prestory helps generate strong dramatic tension when the movie opens.

And here is when it gets to be fun: In the first comic sequence, the writer is always ahead of the audience. That doesn't happen often in the movies. You want to enter the action from page one, word one. So make sure something has happened before the movie has opened.

EXAMPLES: In *Superbad,* high school is ending. The teens are going off to college. Evan (Michael Cera) has been accepted at Dartmouth. So has Fogell "McLovin" (Christopher Mintz-Plasse). They have not told Seth (Jonah Hill.) We don't see the acceptance into college. It has happened before the movie opens.

In *There's Something About Mary,* here's the prestory: Ted (Ben Stiller) cannot get a date for the prom. He likes Mary (Cameron Diaz), but she is dating someone named Woogie. When the movie opens, we know something is already in progress.

In *The Hangover,* a wedding is about to happen. The trip to Vegas has already been planned.

And we don't see any of this. We learn this information as the opening comic sequence plays out. The prestory allows the writer to hit the ground running. And that is what you want to do.

So think about what is happening in your character before the story opens.

HOW TO BREAK YOUR STORY

Eight sequences.

Eight pages.

Nothing more.

It's been my experience in writing screenplays and teaching that if the screenplay doesn't work on the logline, on one page, in eight pages, then it will not work in 110 pages.

We start with five cards in each sequence. Those cards will translate to one page of prose, which will translate to roughly thirteen pages of screenplay. We start with the cards/events.

Let's write a movie...

OPEN WITH A HOOK — FIRST IMPRESSIONS

You are looking to draw the reader into the story as soon as possible. You want to begin with a "hook," something that will grab the reader. Since this is a comedy, you want to start with a laugh. A guffaw. A smile.

Remember this is where you are well ahead of the readers. Let them play catch up.

Everyone remembers the opening of *Raiders of the Lost Ark*. We are in a jungle in South America. A man is on an expedition. He's good with a whip. It's scary. It's fun and it's the first scene of the movie. Action movies tend to start with action scenes — establishing the tone. Comedy action movies like *Men in Black* begin with an action scene. *Austin Power* begins with an action scene. *School of Rock* opens at a concert that establishes Dewey (Jack Black) as an over-the-top, self-appointed rock star who is not as good as he thinks.

It's all about tone. The opening pages of a screenplay establish the tone of the story. That is, we know what kind of comedy we are reading/watching. The screenplay for a coming-of-age screenplay like *Adventureland* is going to read much differently that the screenplay for *Wedding Crashers*.

One is a character-driven comedy. The other is a broad comedy.

The opening of *Wedding Crashers* begins with a divorcing couple fiercely arguing in front of our mediators, Jeremy and John.

When your screenplay opens, you want readers to feel they have walked into a great party. Your characters should be in the middle of an action. Something is already going on in their lives.

Have you ever noticed how movies tend to open with an event? Begin with a beginning, *stories have beginnings or endings to start them off.*

The Woody Allen classic *Hannah and Her Sisters* opens with a birthday party. *Sleepless in Seattle* opens with a funeral. In *As Good As It Gets,* a party is going on next door as Melvin Udall is finishing his romance novel.

Let's look at the opening of *The Hangover.* We are in the desert. A car has crashed. The men seem like they have been through hell. This scene is intercut with images of a beautiful bride in her beautiful home waiting for her beautiful wedding. Phil (Bradley Cooper) makes the call he has been dreading and informs the bride that they have lost the groom. A great hook. Why? It's funny. Inappropriately so. But it also asks questions.

- What happened to the groom?
- Will they find the groom?
- Will the couple get married?

> The more questions you can build into the story, the more your reader will be engaged. You want to create the I-have-to-find-out-what-happens-next read.

As for *The Hangover* — pretty good hook. The tone is established. Remember, it's about showing the reader you are in command of the movie. You can set the tone.

SOME OPENING DEVICES YOU CAN USE

Many different devices have been used and re-used throughout film history. If you're stuck for an opening, try one of these:

NARRATION

A movie can open with narration. This opening is when we are hearing the voice of an all-knowing narrator. Someone is telling us a story. That someone is not part of the story.

The movie *500 Days of Summer* opens with a narrator telling the audience this is a story of boy meets girl. The narrator guides us through the first few pages of the screenplay — and, more importantly, sets up the tone of the story.

Voice Over

A voice over is different from a narrator, as it is one of the characters telling the story. A voice over helps to establish character and comedic vision. By hearing the opening thoughts of the protagonist, we immediately get it. We know the person we are going to be spending time with.

There's Something About Mary opens with Ted's voice over. He tells us how he feels about Mary. It's worth noting that the credit sequence features Jonathan Richman singing about Mary. This guitar-playing narrator was used years before in the western-comedy *Cat Ballou*. *There's Something About Mary* uses the voiceover singing talents of Richmond through the movie.

Jerry Maguire also opens with a voice over, as Jerry the Agent, tells us everything about his life. It continues over the entire first sequence. We know how Jerry is feeling, what is bothering him. We know the tone. If you watch *The Apartment,* you might notice that the voice over is very similar to the voice over in *Jerry Maguire.* Both are men, Jerry and C.C. Baxter (Jack Lemmon). Both men talk about the world, the building they work in, and what they do. It is pretty much the same opening.

This is not called stealing; it is homage. Writer-director Cameron Crowe loves the films of Billy Wilder, so he emulates, pays tribute. Writers love movies and sometimes pay tribute by nodding to something that came before. Take a look at Sally in *When Harry Met Sally* and Annie from *Annie Hall.* They seem to have the same fashion consultant.

Frame Story

Sometimes you are telling a frame story. The framing device began in the novel form with *Wuthering Heights* and *Frankenstein.* It is a story within a story. It usually is someone looking back on his or her life. The baseball comedy *A League of Their Own* opens with Dottie (Geena Davis) preparing to visit the Hall of Fame. The movie then shows us her life as a young woman playing professional baseball. It ends with Dottie, in present day at the Hall of Fame. The story is framed.

The Hangover uses a variation of the frame story. As mentioned, it opens with Phil calling the bride. We return to this scene about fifteen minutes before the end of the movie, specifically at the end of Sequence G.

PROLOGUE

Movies sometimes open with a prologue, which is different from the prestory. It is used a lot when events from the past are very important to the story taking place in the now. It is a short event from the past that establishes the characters at a different time. The entire opening sequence of *There's Something About Mary* is a prologue. It's all about high school and what happens on prom night. It has a beginning, a middle, and an end. The story picks up years later.

Prologues might show us the lives of the characters when they were younger, dramatizing how their personalities were forged at an early age. *Broadcast News* is a romantic comedy about a very opinionated network producer (Holly Hunter), a nebbish writer in love with her (Albert Brooks), and a very dumb, but handsome anchorman/journalist (William Hurt). The movie opens by showing them as kids: We see the young network producer arguing with her Dad about his poor choice of words; we see the young (even for high school) writer condemning his classmates as he delivers a graduation speech and then gets beaten up; and we see a young, good looking boy who is failing at school and doesn't know what skills he might have in life. Subtitled under his name: Future Anchorman.

The classic Bruce Jay Friedman/Brian Grazer and Ganz and Mandel script *Splash* opens with a prologue in Cape Cod as we meet Tom Hanks as a boy, falling into the water and meeting the mermaid. As discussed in the character chapter, sometimes the prologue can be used to show the hero's ghost; the event that still haunts the main character.

In the movie, *Honeymoon in Vegas*, Jack (played by Nick Cage) visits his dying mother in the hospital; she makes him promise never to get married. This promise haunts Jack, sets up the comedic tone of the movie, and opens with an event.

MONTAGE

A montage is a series of short scenes united by a common theme or idea, showing us the main character or characters of the movie. It might be set to music. It is visual. (*Team America*, anyone?) *The 40-Year-Old Virgin* opens with a montage showing us the life of Andy. It's a series of scenes showing him waking up with erections, living alone, playing video games, collecting toys. *Four Weddings and a Funeral* opens with a montage built around our main characters waking up for a wedding — except Charlie (Hugh Grant) who wakes up late.

Always remember tone: *The 40-Year-Old Virgin* montage signals broad comedy; the *Four Weddings and a Funeral* montage communicates romantic comedy.

Montages might be all about character. *Tootsie* opens with a montage. It is not a throw away. It actually can set up a lot about the character. As the montage of *Tootsie* ends, we have learned that Michael is a very good actor; he can't get work; he argues with directors; he has a temper, and there is gender confusion in the movie. It is also funny.

Regardless of which opening device you use, if any at all, what you need to do is establish the world. When we say "the world," we don't always mean a world that might be found in another galaxy or a fantasy world; it's the world in which your story will take place. It can be a college reunion. A small town. A fishing village. The suburbs. Don't just tell us the city. They are all different.

A Scene

Of course, your story can open with a scene introducing your characters. But how you introduce your characters is just as important as how you choose to open the movie.

TAKE A CARD

Take a blank index card. Write down your idea for the opening. Let's say your hero is a pizza chef. MONTAGE — MAKING PIZZA is all you need to write.

Place that card on the top left of your corkboard. You are going to be building eight columns of five cards each.

DEFINING ACTION

Your next card/event is **defining action.** "Character is action" is an age-old maxim. Simply put: You see a man in a suit waiting at a bus stop, you have no idea who he is. You see that same man digging into the garbage can for something to eat; we get who he is and what kind of situation he might be in.

You never want to introduce your protagonist simply by having her talk to someone else about what is going on in her life. You want *to show* what is going on in her life. This is the *defining action.* What is the first action we see that defines your character? If your protagonist appears in that opening hook, make sure you tell us what he is doing when we meet him in that opening.

The opening scene is often combined with the defining action. In *Wedding Crashers,* Jeremy and John are not just introduced as divorce mediators. They are shown as being really good at what they do — they can spin tales, make jokes, they are a team.

Little Miss Sunshine introduces all of its characters with clear defining actions that quickly establish who they are and that contrast with who they are at the end of the movie. But for now, let's look at who they are when the movie opens and how clear their defining actions are:

- Olive Hoover is watching a beauty contest on VHS.
- Richard Hoover is giving a self-help seminar to a sparse classroom.
- Dwyane is doing push-ups in his ambition to join the air force.
- Grandpa is shooting heroin.
- Sheryl is driving, smoking, frantic — the one trying to hold the family together.
- Frank Ginsberg is despondent in a hospital chair recovering from an attempted suicide.

Within two minutes of screen time we know who everyone is!

Remember: Never under-estimate the importance of what a character is doing when we first meet him. When we first meet Jerry in *Jerry Maguire*, he is the shark in a suit, making deals, and commanding attention. Ted in *There's Something About Mary* has braces, he seems a little dorky, and is accepting a "maybe" from a girl he asked out to the prom.

If you are not sure how to introduce your protagonist, remember his or her pole-to-pole transformation. Think of who they are at the end of the story and contrast it at the beginning. Flip it. You are always looking for characters to go on an emotional journey that transforms them into something different.

TAKE A CARD

Take another blank index card. Write down what you see as the *defining action* for your main character. This is the second card in the first sequence.

STATUS QUO — SOMETHING'S MISSING

What you want to do in the first sequence, and the first act of your screenplay, is show the audience two main components of character. The first thing you want to show is *the status quo* of your protagonist. Basically it's the current state of affairs in your protagonist's life. It's very important that you show us what life would be like if the movie didn't happen. That means, if the tornado hadn't hit Kansas, and Dorothy hadn't landed over the rainbow, what would her life have been like? We know it would have been in black and white.

If Jerry Maguire hadn't written the mission statement that led to his being fired because he cares, his life would have stayed on the same course. He would be the head of an agency. He would have married Avery.

Richard Hoover in *Little Miss Sunshine* is trying to convince himself and others that success only comes from winning. He doesn't connect with his family yet. He learns a lesson when Olive goes to the Little Miss Sunshine contest. If he hadn't gone to the contest, there is a good chance his family would have disintegrated into divorce and despair.

That is the status quo. In a few minutes, something is going to happen to disrupt that status quo and your protagonist is going to try and restore life to the way it was.

You also want to set up a protagonist who has *something missing* in their life. Whether they realize it is up to you. But the audience needs to be made aware that there is a hole in their heart, in their life — they are not a complete person. It is okay for your protagonist to express a yearning for something more. We want to know that *something is missing* in their lives. In teen comedies, the protagonist may be graduating and has not had sex yet. It might be love.

In *The Hangover,* the groom is a pretty happy guy. But what about his groomsmen? Alan feels alone. He yearns to connect with the wolf pack and be accepted by his brother-in-law as a real brother. Phil hates his job; he doesn't want to get stuck with his wife and kids. He is stealing money from school children to fund his fun in Vegas. And Stu the Dentist is picked on by his girlfriend who has cheated on him. He has to lie to her about where he is going. Something is clearly missing.

In *Old School,* Mitch, Frank, and Beanie are long past their college days. Since the movie opens with Mitch (Luke Wilson) and he is the one who moves into the house that becomes the fraternity, the story is his. Beanie (Vince Vaughn) and Frank the Tank (Will Ferrell) have clear story arcs and beginnings, middles, and ends, but Mitch is the Godfather of the frat house. At the end of the movie, Mitch and Nicole (Ellen Pompeo) are a couple. Love is what is missing in Mitch's life. When we meet him, his wife Heidi (Juliette Lewis) is in the middle of having a very risqué affair.

The status quo of your story is a comedic world. Your characters should exist in a world that will generate laughs. How to generate laughs comes from you, how you see the world. I once began a seminar on comedy writing by saying, "If you had a good time in high school, you can leave now." Seriously. How do you see your world? Your job? Your life? If you see your children as perfect little angels — that's awesome. Chances are you're not seeing them with a comedic vision. If you see them as money-sucking, time-wasting parasites from another world — note that I can relate. Yes, I am exaggerating. That's what comedy is.

How do you visualize what is missing? In *West Side Story,* Tony sings about it. If you're writing a musical, then it's easy. What you need is a *Greek Chorus*. In ancient Greek plays, the Greek Chorus would comment on the action. (If you want to see the comedic version of a Greek Chorus, watch *Mighty Aphrodite*). You need to make use of a Greek Chorus of friends to whom your protagonist or antagonist can talk. Why? That Greek Chorus stands in for the audience. The Greek Chorus also gives your good guy or bad guy someone to talk to. Did you ever notice when one character will turn to another character in a movie and say, "Do you know what your problem is?" That is how *we* find out what is missing in the hero's life.

TAKE A CARD

Take another blank index card. What is missing in your protagonist's life?

EXPOSITION

The exposition scenes are the "once upon a time" scenes in the movies. They are telling who, what, when, where, and why we are here. Only deliver exposition as needed. What is important to know at the beginning of the movie? Save the big dramatic reveals for later. All you are doing now is showing us the regular life of the protagonist. We want to know the world in which your main character lives.

Let's look at *Knocked Up*. We meet Ben Stone in a montage, smoking pot, acting like a kid. He has no job. He wants to create a web site that categorizes the nude scenes of famous actresses. Then we meet Allison. She is living with her sister. She works at the "E" network and her career is on the rise. These were interesting meets for both of them. We have learned what we need to know to get the story going. We know they are two very different people.

That is all we need to know at this point. We don't need to know how Ben has money to live — that comes later. We don't need to know about Allison's sister's problems — again, later. We know that they are opposites on a collision course.

> **TAKE A CARD**
>
> Take another blank index card. What exposition is needed in your story now? What can you tell us about your protagonist? What is the best way to show it? How is exposition revealed in your reference movies?

POINT OF ATTACK — OPPORTUNITY KNOCKS

SOMETHING HAPPENS

Now that you have written these scenes in paragraph form, you have an idea of what is happening. You have introduced some of the characters. You may have introduced your antagonist and some of the subplot characters. You are setting the table.

We know whom the story is going to be about. The next time you're at a movie, pay extra attention to the first ten minutes. It's all about character. And then something happens to our hero. Dramatists have given this moment many names: inciting event, inciting incident, turning point, point of attack. I call it *opportunity knocks.*

The protagonist thinks his or her life is moving along fine when something happens. They don't want to be bothered — but they are. Something disrupts their perfectly laid plans.

- Something happens that disrupts the status quo of their lives
- Something happens that they have to deal with
- Something happens that gets the story moving

Do not confuse this moment with the end of the first act. We don't know what the screenplay/movie is about yet. We don't know the main dramatic action. This moment is what leads to the end of the first act.

Big events in your screenplay are connected. The moment at the end of the first sequence insures that the end of the first act takes place. For example, in *Superbad,* the guys are invited to the party. This event leads to their wild night of buying — or attempting to buy — booze.

In *Old School,* Mitch Martin (Luke Wilson) moves into a house right near campus. Opportunity is knocking. He doesn't know it but his life will never be the same.

Everything that comes after the "opportunity knocks" moment is cause and effect.

This precise moment/event leads to a series of events.

In *Shrek,* all Shrek wants is to be left alone. He lives a solitary life, but when fairytale creatures arrive in his swamp, he suddenly has to deal with others. The fairytale creatures arriving in his swamp is the "something happens" moment. He doesn't realize it's an opportunity to change his life and fall in love. He hates this intrusion.

In *Tootsie,* the "something happens" moment happens when Michael learns about Sandy's audition for the role of Emily Brewster. He agrees to help her. Michael agrees to accompany her to the audition. Going to that audition changes his life forever.

This last card/event is the end of the first comic sequence. A change has happened to the protagonist from when we first met him or her. The scenes in your first column should have a beginning, middle, and an end. Think of the last card in the sequence as having the words: **TO BE CONTINUED...**

That is what you are trying to convey. The sense of wondering: What is going to happen next?

In *Jerry Maguire*, Jerry's mission statement is delivered. He thinks his life has begun. We hear two agents asking, how long does he have? They give him a week.

We know more than the main character. We know his world is beginning to unravel. He doesn't know it yet; we do. If Jerry doesn't write the mission statement — no movie.

If Ted in *Something About Mary* doesn't get the "frank and beans" in the zipper, no movie. He is never haunted by Mary. In *Knocked Up,* if Ben Stone doesn't meet Allison, he doesn't have a one-night stand with her. There's no baby. No movie.

Something has to happen — and it's time. We have learned all we need to know. It's time to get the plot going.

TO DO:

You have your first row of cards. Now, on one page, using the CARD HEADINGS as a guideline, write out the action happening in that section. You are writing in prose. AVOID DIALOGUE. Save that for when you write the script. Right now, you are writing to tell the story. It has to be only one page with proper margins and proper font size. If it goes over — trim it down.

Do you open visually? Comically?

Have you introduced the protagonist in an interesting way?

Is there a strong "opportunity knocks" moment?

● EXERCISE: REWRITE YOUR FAVORITE MOVIE

In this chapter, we have talked about different types of opening devices for movies. I want you to imagine you have been hired to rewrite your favorite comedy of all time — but the studio wants it to open differently.

So write the first three pages of the screenplay for *your favorite produced movie.* You have to use the same characters. You have to have the same tone. You have to be telling the same story but you have to tell it differently.

What if *Ghostbusters* opens with a prequel? Imagine Drs. Venkman, Stantz, and Spengler are friends at camp together when they see their first ghost? Could be funny.

Or, what if *Knocked Up* is told with a voiceover from the unborn baby talking about what a loser his dad is?

Have fun. Be liberating. It's a go movie!

CHAPTER SIX

COMIC SEQUENCE (B)

SETTING UP THE INAPPROPRIATE GOAL

A.K.A "YOU'RE GOING TO DO WHAT?" OR

WHY CRASHING A WEDDING IS A GOOD IDEA

NASCAR RULE OF ACT ONE

The *first half* of Act One deals with character. The *second half* is going to deal with plot and setting up the *inappropriate goal*. That's what the next sequence is for. That's what the next column of cards will be for.

The audience has settled in. Had a few laughs. But we're not in a sketch, we're in a movie, and they want to know what the story is going to be about. Don't confuse the point of attack with the end of the first act.

In the first half of Act One, we meet the driver.

In the second half of Act One, we build the car.

At the end of Act One, we put the gas in the tank. It's where the story gets going.

Right now, let's build the car.

The "opportunity knocks" moment upsets the everyday existence of the comic character but it does not get the story going.

Since this is a comedy, in Act Two the wheels will fall off. Literally. Car destruction is huge in comedy.

Something has just happened that is forever going to change your comic hero's life but he or she doesn't know it yet.

Ben has just met Allison in the bar. Look out!

Think about the last beat you hit at the end of the first sequence — opportunity knocks. Something has upset the apple cart — the protagonist is still getting information. She is not yet at the point of no return (the end of the first act) but she's going to get there soon.

In this section we are still meeting characters and introducing subplots. (Be sure to introduce the antagonist sometime in Act One!) This comic sequence sets up the main tension of the movie. This part is where the audience will learn what the story is really about.

Remember: Each comic sequence has a beginning, middle, and an end. It stands on its own as a comic sequence. A change occurs from who the protagonist was at the beginning of this part of the story to who he is at the end. This point is where you fill the audience in on what the main action of the story is going to be.

JACK IN THE BOX

It is important as you craft your story to develop plants and payoffs. I look at these as jack-in-the-box moments. In Act One, you might place the "box" (the plant) in a scene. Later, in the script, you will return to that and payoff that joke. For example, in *There's Something About Mary*, Ted visits Warren and brings a baseball. He makes the mistake of touching Warren's earmuffs. Warren flips out and beats up Ted. At the end of the movie, when Ted is broken hearted and has to say goodbye, he pulls away Warren's earmuffs. Warren does not attack. He says goodbye sweetly, something that is not lost on Mary.

Just as we identified the five key events of Act One, we will do the same for the next comic sequence.

WHAT THE HELL HAPPENED TO ME?

W/e want to laugh at characters. We want to see the flaws. Oftentimes we will see an *exaggerated response*. It's the *What the hell just happened to me?* moment.

Your comedic hero was going through life as best he could. He had flaws he was dealing with, but for the most part he was *resigned to be who he was*.

If the movie never happens Andy might die an eighty-year-old virgin.

If Ted doesn't get the "frank and beans" caught in his zipper, he might go to prom with Mary and they might hit it off.

But *something did happen* — and comedic characters need to react to that.

> *Movies/screenplays from this point forward are about events and how characters react to the events of the story.*

Having characters reacting to what is happening to them humanizes them to the audience. The audience identifies. Because this movie is a comedy, it's the *comic reaction* that counts. Immediately after Andy is exposed as a virgin in *The 40-Year-Old Virgin,* he reacts. He is panicked. Nervous.

Immediately after Ted gets his zipper caught and is carted away in an ambulance, a reaction scene occurs. When he is wheeled out to the ambulance, Mary is walking alongside him. Ted is valiantly giving the thumbs up to the crowd when the paramedics drop him. Funny. Unless you're Ted, then it's humiliating and painful. But it's not happening to us. That's why it's funny.

The "what the hell happened to me?" event could take place in real time. It could take place ten years later if you are doing a prequel. But the important thing here is that we want to see that moment. We have to.

The audience wants to see how the protagonist deals with these life-altering events. And since it's a comedy, the protagonist often does so in pathetic, comedic fashion.

Andy runs on the street, worried that "they know" his secret.

Ted is seen in therapy, where the only one listening is the audience. The therapist has turned away.

In *Forgetting Sarah Marshall,* something happens when Sarah dumps Peter. He wonders what the hell happened to me? How does he react to this? He messes up at work. He drinks too much. He goes on a string of sex dates. He cries after sex.

TAKE A CARD

How does your protagonist react to what has happened to him?

THE BUDDY

If you haven't introduced him to the audience yet, make sure you bring in the Buddy. This is the best friend. The side-kick. The mentor. Someone who sits in for the audience and asks questions. The Buddy does not have to agree with the protagonist. In fact, it's better that he or she doesn't, as conflict always makes for a better scene.

Remember that Greek Chorus? Time to put it to work. The protagonist needs someone to talk to. In a romantic comedy, it might be the other person. *When Harry Met Sally* makes great use of the comic sequences. The opening sequence is setting up the differences in the characters when Harry and Sally are out of college and driving from Chicago to New York. This drive is where we become aware of their different points of view on friendship and sex. Sequence A ends with them saying goodbye at the arc at Washington Square Park. (A jack-in-the-box moment: Harry is going to be back here later in the movie). The second sequence in the movie is a few years later as Harry and Sally meet on a plane traveling from Washington D.C. to New York. In the opening sequence, Harry is seen kissing his loved one goodbye. He is the one in a relationship. In the second Sequence B, Sally is the one seen kissing a loved one goodbye. She is in a relationship.

They are each other's buddies, but they don't know it.

In *Forgetting Sarah Marshall,* Brian Better (Bill Hader) is always there for Peter (Jason Segal). He speaks to him with candor. Comedic candor. Brian encourages him to take a vacation. He speaks the truth. He calls him; and calls him out, if need be.

TAKE A CARD

Write a buddy scene with your protagonist. Are they talking about what just happened?

MEET THE BAD GUY A.K.A. THE DICK

There's a good chance we have met the bad guy or bad girl in the opening comic sequence of the story. If we haven't, now is a good time. You want to avoid second act introductions as much as possible. When the story gets going in Act Two, you want to know who the players are.

Of course, in a road movie *(Due Date, Euro-Trip, Sullivan's Travels)* your heroes will continually meet new people. That is the point of the trip. But the principals are mostly introduced. That is, stories where the characters will go on a physical journey. *The Hangover* is a road movie. The guys go on a journey looking for Doug. Along the way they are confronted with various forms of "bad guys." But there is conflict in Act One. They are not sure that Alan (Zach Galifiankis) can be trusted. Stu (Ed Helms) has to deal with his horrible girlfriend.

You want to make sure you have a worthy antagonist for your heroes. Who is that speed bump or roadblock on their highway to happiness? Treat your antagonists with respect. They want something, too. They are not just mustache twirlers. Give them a Greek Chorus with whom to converse. Make them a real threat to our hero.

Jerry Maguire has Bob Sugar (Jay Mohr), who is stealing his clients. He is not in a lot of the movie but Bob Sugar appears at key dramatic moments: when Jerry is fired, when he loses his star client, and at the final game when Jerry and Rod are redeemed.

In *There's Something About Mary*, Ted hires Healy (Matt Dillon), who will turn into his nemesis. He is the one who is keeping Ted from his goal.

In *Forgetting Sarah Marshall*, the bad guy is not the British rock star Aldus Snow. It is Sarah Marshall. Peter wants to forget her and he can't. But it's not easy when she is having sex right next door!

In *Wedding Crashers*, the bad guy is Zachary "Sack" Lodge, Claire's boyfriend and potential fiancé.

Sometimes the enemy is thine own self. In *As Good As It Gets*, the enemy is the mental illness from which Melvin Udall (Jack!) suffers. In *Liar, Liar*, the enemy is a lie. Or, it can be a curse as in *Groundhog Day*.

The forces of antagonism need to be strong and cannot be defeated until the end of the movie. In romantic comedies, the bad guy tends to be the other person in the relationship. How are the forces of antagonism defeated in a romantic comedy? With love. The couple winds up together.

TAKE A CARD
Introduce the BAD GUY

ALL CHARACTERS THINK THEY ARE THE STAR

Every character believes that he or she is the star of the movie. They think the story is happening to them. Mitch (Luke Wilson) is the protagonist in Old School. *The story starts with him and he is the character that goes through the biggest emotional change. However, don't tell that to Frank the Tank (Will Ferrell). He thinks it's his movie. He gets married, gets divorced. Or, what about Beanie (Vince Vaughn)? He realizes he loves his wife. Wait? Dean Gordon (Jeremy Piven) thinks it's his movie. He wants nothing more than to get even with the guys who tortured him in college. Make a list of your characters — decide what they want. They are not just there to service the plot... they are all on their own journeys.*

THE DRAMATIC QUESTION — OH, THAT'S WHAT IT'S ABOUT

Today's audiences are patient, but not as patient as they used to be. Today's audiences have been assaulted with trailers that give away every plot point. The movie has been over-marketed. They already have an idea of what is going to happen when they sit in their seats and start eating their popcorn.

So far we have enjoyed meeting the characters and laughing at them. But now, we are ready for the main action of the story to begin.

A certain pacing is inherent to mainstream Hollywood movies. Around seventeen minutes into the movie (give or take a few), we get a hint of what the movie is going to be about.

You don't believe me? The next time you're watching a DVD, take a look at the counter. Around the seventeen-minute mark the *dramatic question* is introduced. *This is not the end of the first act.* If anything, it's the beginning of the end of the first act.

It doesn't happen on the tick of the clock. Sixteen minutes. Eighteen minutes. Something happens that lets us know what the movie is going to be about. This moment does not mark the end of the first act. The end of the first act is when the protagonist has a clear objective. But the page seventeen mark informs the audience and protagonist what we're in store for and what the script is going to be dealing with over the next ninety pages.

The following are roughly the seventeen-minute mark of various movies.

Forgetting Sarah Marshall
The end of the first section (A) was when Sarah dumped Peter. Now Peter is dealing with the fallout and he is not doing well. His best friend tells him to take a vacation. Peter goes to Hawaii and, around seventeen minutes in, learns that he is at the same resort as Sarah Marshall! The woman he is trying to forget!

Anchorman
Ron Burgundy (Will Ferrell) has met the beautiful Veronica Corningstone (Christina Applegate) at the end of section A, now he learns she is going to be working with him.

Wedding Crashers
Jeremy and John have decided to crash the biggest wedding ever (end of A). Around seventeen minutes in John meets Claire (Rachel McAdams). It is what the story is about.

Bridget Jones's Diary
Bridget attends the book launch and runs into Mark Darcy (Colin Firth).

The Hangover
The guys wake up in the trashed hotel room and can't find Doug. They haven't decided to begin the search for Doug. They just realize he is missing.

The dramatic question is when the protagonist is introduced to the main action of the story.

> **TAKE A CARD**
>
> What event introduces the dramatic question of story?

END OF THE FIRST ACT — PROTAGONIST AND OBJECTIVE

As we approach the end of the first act, the protagonist is at the point of no return. It is time to go on the journey. *After this event* the protagonist will never be the same: It is impossible. Something dramatic has happened.

Every movie is asking a major question and here is where the question of the movie is established. What happens at the end of Act One emerges from the *dramatic question* introduced in the story.

So a *major question* has been posed. At the end of Act One of the following comedy blockbusters, we are asking:

Forgetting Sarah Marshall
Will Peter forget Sarah even though he has decided to stay at the same hotel?

Anchorman
Will Ron and Veronica make it as a couple and will he learn to respect her as a peer?

Wedding Crashers
What is going to happen now that Jeremy and John have broken their code and are staying at the McCreary's house? Will John win the girl?

Bridget Jones's Diary
Whom will Bridget end up with?

Answering the question is the fun of the movie. It's why you are writing the screenplay. It is a question that will not be answered until you type "FADE OUT."

ESTABLISH THE WANT

If the first sequence was about the driver of your car, and the second sequence was about building the car, then the end of the first act is about putting the gas into that car. Your protagonist must have a goal or there will be no gas in the engine. The car won't go. Your story won't go.

Remember we talked about how movies are about how *someone wants something and is having trouble getting it?* You better establish the "want." The audience members need a clear idea of where the journey is taking them.

What is happening to the main character is the *most important thing to happen in the character's life,* although he or she might not know it yet. They are about to begin a journey to find out who they really are.

You cannot continue until you know what your main character wants!

VISUALIZE THE END OF THE FIRST ACT

The hero begins his/her journey. He is now crossing into a new world, toward a new goal. His life has been disrupted and this is the only chance he has to return it to the status quo that was established in Act One. How do you show this?

Film is a visual medium. Action is character. Jerry Maguire walking out of the office is a crossing. It shows us Jerry leaving one world and crossing into another.

In the timeless comedy blockbuster *Back to the Future,* Marty McFly drives in the time machine from 1985 to 1955. A crossing.

The journey has begun for your protagonist.

The journey is beginning for you.

TAKE A CARD

Add five more cards to your corkboard.

Are you thinking of scenes in terms of events?

Are things happening to your main character?

On another page, write out the action of Sequence B.

If you need to go back and make changes to the first sequence, do it. But don't get stuck there. Writing is rewriting. Even now you will be rewriting your cards/events. You will be rewriting your treatment.

But you don't want to get stuck in the past — let's keep moving forward.

● EXERCISE: CHANGE THE POINT OF VIEW

Your screenplay is going to need a strong opponent to succeed. It's only as good as the bad guy or the bad girl in the movie who is there to give your protagonist a hard time. But you can't have them just be a mustache twirler, a clichéd villain. They have to want something that the hero is preventing them from getting. They have to have a reason to despise the hero.

You have to be that bad guy.

On one page, write in your antagonist's voice what they want and why they don't like the protagonist. For example, if you were doing this for the movie *Goldfinger*, think of Auric Goldfinger as the good guy and James Bond as the bad guy.

"Damn that, Bond! Things were great until he showed up with his good looks and his way with women. The gold belongs to me. He's the narcissist with the gun, not me!"

Tell the story from the bad guy's point of view.

If you're doing a romantic comedy, do both lovers — how they feel about each other and, most importantly, why they think they are right!

CHAPTER SEVEN

ACT TWO!

A.K.A. WHERE SCRIPTS GO TO DIE

COMIC SEQUENCE (C)

THE MAD, MAD, MAD, MAD WORLD

A.K.A. SOMETIMES GIRLS THROW UP ON YOU

Welcome to Act Two! Otherwise known as the next fifty to sixty pages of your screenplay. The place where scripts go to die. It's the hardest part of the script to write.

But, remember, Act Two is just four shorter movies.

Each sequence is built around a specific goal. A smaller objective. It's not that scary. Act Two is where you stick your character up a tree and throw rocks.

We continue with the comedic sequences, naming it The Mad, Mad, Mad, Mad World as an homage to the classic comedy from the 1960s

Before getting into specific events that go into this next sequence, let's discuss Act Two as a whole.

It will be divided into two halves. Act Two-A and Act Two-B. Remember: It's all equal. If your first sequence was fifteen pages, all of your sequences will wind up around fifteen pages.

OH YES, OH NO!

Remember in Act One, you asked some sort of question — a dramatic/thematic question:

Will Harry and Sally get together?

Can men and women sleep together and still be friends?

Will Greg ever propose to Pam in *Meet the Parents?*

Act Two is where you are going to go back and forth on the outcome of that answer. We should wonder how the main dramatic question is going to be answered. To keep the outcome in doubt, the rest of your screenplay should be filled with OH YES moments and OH NO moments.

Example — *School of Rock*

Dewey wants to be in a great rock-and-roll band. He wants to be discovered and recognized for the rock God that only he knows he is.

OH NO!

Dewey is teaching at a private school.

OH YES!

Dewey is teaching these kids to play rock.

OH NO!

Dewey is found out. He is not a real music teacher. He is fired.

OH YES!

The kids really want to compete in the battle of the bands.

OH NO!

They lose the battle of the bands.

OH YES!

Dewey discovers who he really is, what he is really good at it. He becomes a great music teacher at his newly formed school of rock.

Back and forth you will go throughout the rest of the screenplay. Is it going to work out? Is it going to fail? Ted and Mary are falling in love (yes!). But all these other guys want her (no!)

In *Wedding Crashers,* John and Claire are falling in love (yes!), but she finds out he is lying (no!)

You have to be prepared for your hero to lose.

You will not answer the main question of the movie until the end. You are going to take the reader/audience for a ride. They should always be in doubt about the outcome of the answer to the question. They know it's a comedy so chances are the protagonist will win out, find love, and be happy. But that is not why we go to the movies. We go to see *how* the protagonist is going to win out, find love, and be happy... and laugh along the way.

Start Small and Go Big

A very simple rule about Act Two: Start small and go big. There's not as much at stake at the beginning of Act Two as there will be by the end of Act Two. By the end of Act Two, usually more people will be involved: The protagonist will have more to lose now. The jeopardy will have increased.

Flirting with Disaster begins with Mel (Ben Stiller) wanting to find his birth parents. At the beginning of Act Two, he starts off on the journey with his wife and the woman from the adoption agency. By the end of Act Two, Ben is with his wife, the woman from the adoption agency, the baby, his birth parents, two FBI agents, an acid-loving step-brother, and his real parents. Whew!

Old School starts out with Mitch (Luke Wilson) needing a place to live. By the end of Act Two the fraternity has grown — a lot more people are involved.

THE PROMISE OF THE PREMISE

If you're being dramatic, this is where you want the drama.

If you're writing an action movie — KA-BOOM.

If you're writing a comedy, this is where you need to get the laughs.

You've enticed us with the logline, hooked us with the opening, set up the characters and the situation, and now the fun begins. In Act Two, you have to deliver it.

The first comedy screenplay I co-wrote was called *Verona.* The producer involved read it, liked it, and then decided I didn't have enough trailer moments. "What are those?" I wondered. He said: "When you lie in bed at night and think of your movie, and you imagine the trailer in your head — what do you see?"

What are the big, sustained set pieces in your movie?

What visuals do you see when you imagine your movie?

Write them down.

THE MAIN EVENTS OF SEQUENCE C

THE MAD, MAD, MAD, MAD WORLD

I'm calling this section The Mad, Mad, Mad, Mad World for a reason. Something different has now happened in your story — or should have. Usually this change happens about twenty-four to thirty minutes in. Spec scripts today are around the twenty-four to twenty-seven-page mark. Everything that happened in Act One is considered the ordinary world. Everything that happens now in the second act is the special world, different.

In our comedic structure — it's the mad, mad, mad, mad world.

The protagonist is walking into a new place. A new situation. The end of Act One was a game changer. The protagonist's life has changed dramatically. He or she is reacting to that change. So even if the location has not changed — something has. To pay tribute to *The Apartment:*

Emotion-wise.

Location-wise.

Situation-wise.

It can be a new special world of love. A new world an enemy has entered. The mad, mad, mad, mad world contrasts with everything that was before.

In *The 40-Year-Old Virgin,* the mad, mad, mad, mad world for Andy is a world in which his friends know his secret and he is going to make a huge attempt to lose his virginity. The location has not changed but the emotion has.

In *Little Miss Sunshine,* the Hoover family has decided to hit the road and take Olive to the Little Miss Sunshine pageant. The location has changed.

In *Tropic Thunder,* the actors think they are acting in a movie and set off to find the set. They believe they are being filmed. The audience is in on the joke. They know it's a real situation in a hostile environment, but the actors don't. Even though we are in the same part of the world with the same people, something is new — the situation.

In *The Hangover,* the guys have realized Doug is missing. They begin looking for him, piecing together the clues of what happened the night before. The world without Doug is the new mad, mad, mad, mad world.

Remember *When Harry Met Sally* — what has changed when Act Two-A begins? Harry and Sally have. It's clearly established that they both are now single. Harry's wife moved out. Joe and Sally have each broken up. They are single, in the city — let the games begin.

In romantic comedies, this new world is where the couple starts courting.

PEOPLE ARE LAZY — AND SO IS YOUR PROTAGONIST

At the end of Act One, your protagonist has encountered a huge problem. He or she has set off on a journey with a clear goal. They've made a decision to correct the imbalance in their world and restore the status quo. They have a problem that needs fixing...

When you have a problem that needs fixing, what do you do? You do the easiest, simplest thing possible. You always look for the quickest, easiest solution.

THE GOAL OF THE NEXT SEQUENCE

To find the easiest way to fix the problem, you always look for the easy way out. So will your protagonist. Because he is lazy.

Avoid being episodic.

When someone calls your script *episodic,* he is not being kind. It means the script was a series of scenes/events that appeared in no real order. You want to create a structure that is cause and effect. One thing happens, which leads to another thing happening.

If you card out your screenplay in forty cards (eight columns of five cards each), you will be able to lean back and see if one event leads to another. It should. Chances are if a scene can be moved to anywhere in the script, it doesn't belong *anywhere* in the script. Adjust it. Change it. Rework it so it is necessary and has to be in there.

Establish the Initial Goal

The best way to avoid being episodic is to tell the audience/reader what is going on. What does the protagonist want? How do they plan to get it? What do they need to do at this moment in the story? What does the protagonist need to do to solve his problem? How will they go about it? Put yourself in their shoes. Imagine the situation.

Little Miss Sunshine is a road movie. The road is going to slow the Hoovers down. They set out on their journey the easiest way they can. They hop into their iconic yellow minivan and head west, driving toward the beauty pageant. That seems easy enough. Then the car breaks down and the minigoal becomes to fix the car.

Jerry Maguire declares at the end of the first act that he is going to start his own agency. He's on his own. He has one client, Rod, whom he is not even sure he wants. He has a star client, Cushman. Cushman is the potential number one pick in the upcoming NFL draft. Jerry knows that if he can keep Cushman, he is back. Avery, his girlfriend, reminds him that he doesn't have to be a loser. Jerry makes the decision to go get Cushman as a client. He's not worried about the overall goal of starting his own agency and becoming very successful. That doesn't matter now. All that matters now is that he gets Cushman.

Each sequence has a beginning of the sequence, a middle, and an end. The end of the sequence spins the story into another direction. Usually what happens is the protagonist does not achieve the initial goal, which leads to more complications; or, if the protagonist achieves the mini goal, that leads to a different problem.

As a writer, you are always living in the moment with these characters. You, the author, know how the story is going to end. But your audience doesn't. So try occupying their skin for a moment. Think like they will think.

LEARNING NEW RULES / TAKING ON APPEARANCES

If you go to a foreign country, you ask questions. You want to learn the rules. Your friends come over with a new board game. You don't just sit down and play, you have to learn how to play. What are the rules? This learning is happening for your protagonist.

Your protagonist is learning about a new situation, a new relationship, new rules — and the audience should be learning with her. This is a key event/beat that happens very early on in Act Two-A.

In *Honeymoon in Vegas,* Jack has been set up to lose at poker. He doesn't know that. All Jack knows is that he owes a lot of money to a gangster. He is in the mad, mad, mad, mad world of debt. Talk about a movie to which writers can relate! Sonny, the gambler, explains the rules to him and how Jack can get out of debt if he allows his girlfriend to have dinner with the gambler. Complex, but clear.

In *City Slickers,* the first act is all about three friends from New York who yearn for adventure. Mitch is having personal problems. He hates his job. He has lost his smile. He agrees to go with his friends and play cowboy for a week. When he gets to cowboy camp he learns the rules. Someone is explaining them to him and to us. This is how you get to be a cowboy and this is what we're going to do.

TAKING ON APPEARANCES

In this sequence, sometimes a hero will take on a disguise or an attitude that is different. Mitch the Cowboy immediately goes shopping in the beginning of Act Two-A and dresses like a cowboy. That's a very clear new appearance. In the science fiction comedy blockbuster *Galaxy Quest,* Taggert and the crew are on a real spaceship taking on the appearance of their fictional characters. In *Tootsie,* Michael Dorsey dresses as a woman. A new appearance.

Comedies often have deception; someone is lying. In *Oceans 11,* Danny Ocean says this is not about getting Tess back. He is lying. That is all it's about.

Lying is not just a key component in politics. It's in comedy. Usually in a comedy someone is lying about something. *School of Rock?* Dewey is pretending to be his roommate so he can substitute teach, get money, and keep his rock-and-roll dreams alive. *Dave?* Dave is pretending to be the President while the real evil President is in a coma. In *Wedding Crashers,* Jeremy and John pretend to be maple syrup manufacturers.

The point is the protagonist is acting in a different way. A character transformation has begun. Chances are your hero has no idea this is happening to him yet. But by taking on that appearance, he has begun to change.

Friends and Enemies

Throughout the screenplay your protagonist is going to be facing obstacles: speed bumps, road blocks, pies in the face. Anything you can throw at them, throw at them. The battles are going to build. The conflict will escalate as the story progresses.

Lots of times, the protagonist will fail to win these confrontations. That's okay. We want to see people tested. It can be a test of a relationship. A test can be physical. If it's a comedy set in college, the test can be academic.

The hero is not going to be battling the main forces of antagonism for the entire screenplay. It would become redundant.

Ted wants to find Mary in *There's Something About Mary.* Healy is the bad guy. Healy has lied to Ted and told him that Mary is on welfare, in terrible physical and emotional shape, and that Ted should give up on her. Ted still wants to see her. He wants to help. (Talk about heart!). So Ted decides to go drive down to Miami. On the way down, Ted picks up a hitchhiker (who is a serial killer), then he is arrested at a rest-stop, mistaken to be a serial killer and beaten by the police. And all of these events happen in a funny fashion! Healy, the main antagonist, is not slowing Ted down. He has nothing to do with these events.

At this point in your screenplay, we want to see your protagonist confronted. In *The Hangover,* the guys retrieve the police car, go see a doctor (who is not forthcoming with the information), then they are shot at by Mr. Chow's men. A few moments later they will be arrested for stealing that police car. They are used as test dummies in a stun gun demonstration! A little kid tasers them! *The Hangover* is jam-packed with enemies: Mike Tyson, the tiger, the policeman. Ultimately, the guys in *The Hangover* are their own worst enemy.

Nothing ever comes easy.

Along the road you want someone along for the ride — your protagonist will meet new friends or have some old ones along with him. The guys in *The Hangover* make new friends along the way: They find out Stu is married to a stripper named Jade. In *Flirting With Disaster*, Mel is on the road to find his biological parents. He is later joined on the road by Paul and Agent Tony Kent (Richard Jenkins and Josh Brolin).

If you begin to introduce characters, use the unity of opposites. Make them different. There should be a reason they are in the movie. They are not just there to service your plot.

SUBPLOTS

And now a word about subplots. The A plot is the main story. It's the main action of the movie. The main dramatic question. Will the guy get the girl? Will the couple get married? Will the crazy scientists defeat the even crazier alien?

The B plot is the subplot; or the subplots. A subplot receives less emphasis and screen time than the main story but it can elevate your material to new heights. Subplots have their own beginnings, middles, and ends.

Remember we talked about parsing out expostion? Tell us what we need, when we need it. For example, how did Stu lose his tooth in Vegas? The answer is saved for the very end of the movie.

In *The Hangover,* we learn that Stu is married to Jade. This is the beginning of a subplot. The audience wonders what is going to happen to them? This subplot began in Act One when Stu showed his friends the engagement ring. They questioned if he was really serious about marrying Melissa. That was a plant, a jack-in-the-box moment. The ring pays off. In Act Two, Stu finds out he is married to Jade. The audience wonders what is going to happen to Stu and Jade? The screenplay continues to introduce questions that need to be answered. The subplot of Stu and Jade is resolved at the end of the movie. It was a clear dramatic structure that plays out.

In a romantic comedy, the main action of the story might be structured around the subplot. *Sleepless in Seattle* is about a man and a woman falling in love and not meeting until the end of the movie. The subplot of the movie is the article that Annie Reed is writing. It's what moves the plot along.

Can you have multiple subplots? Of course, you can. And all of these subplots have beginnings, middles, and endings.

They start later in the story and have fewer scenes but they are little movies of their own.

Let's look at *Shakespeare in Love*. I am going to list the subplots in the form of a question. If you set-up the subplot with its own dramatic question, you will force yourself to think about how that subplot will get resolved.

When watching *Shakespeare in Love*, we wonder:

- Will Shakespeare finish his play?
- Will the theater close?
- Will Viola get her wish to be an actor?
- Will Viola get married?

And that's all underneath the main plot of "Will and Viola will wind up together." All of these subplots are like mini movies. They have a beginning, a middle, and an end. That's *three events*. Three cards to your board.

COLOR CARDS

I always use different colors for my subplots when carding out my screenplay. So if a subplot is SAVING THE FAMILY BUSINESS, I might make that a green card. I can then add green cards to Act Two and Act Three. I might add more later, but I know that I have to tie up that thread.

A subplot coincides with the main plot line toward the end. They're like trains all arriving at the station around the same time.

SUBPLOTS AND THEMES

W hat else can a subplot do? Subplots can dramatize what the movie is really about. Remember that crazy little thing called theme? As they say in the theater, the subplot needs to be on the spine. It needs to be related to the movie in some way.

For example, in *When Harry Met Sally,* Bruno Kirby and Carrie Fisher's relationship is a subplot that argues against the main plot (Can a man and woman have sex and still be friends?). They have no problem with this idea.

In *Liar, Liar,* Fletcher's court case is the subplot and it shows how lies hurt.

Parenthood explores the theme of what makes a good parent? It's Gil's (Steve Martin) story. The subplots involve his family and their parenting skills.

Let's take a look at the movie *Big,* starring Tom Hanks. *Big* is a movie about a teenager, Josh, who wants to be big and gets his wish — but then he wants to go back. His goal at the end of Act One is to find the fortune-teller machine. But he has to stick it out as an adult. That's a lot of ground to cover. You can't spend the entire movie looking for the fortune-teller machine. Josh has to survive until he finds out where it is. So he has to get a job. Where does Josh work? He works at a toy company. It's a choice that works perfectly with the theme. The adults in the movie are acting like children. Within that main plot of "Will Josh find the fortune-teller machine and get back home?" is the subplot of the romance of Josh and Susan (Elizabeth Perkins). It exists as its own little movie with the movie. Let's break down the Josh/Elizabeth subplot.

- Josh first sees Elizabeth.
- They bump into each other.
- They start to work together.

- They talk at the party. She likes him. They leave together.
- They have a sleepover at Josh's house. She wears his pajamas and sleeps in his bunk bed.
- She takes care of him after a fight and they have their first kiss.
- They have a date at an amusement park.
- At this point, the A plot weaves in — the fortune-teller machine is right there and Josh doesn't notice it.
- They sleep together.
- They break up.
- Josh goes home. Says goodbye to Elizabeth, who believes him.

These scenes are spread out over the course of the movie. Think of what characters you have introduced in your story. How do they wind up at the end? How does their story evolve?

First Attempt Fails — Maybe

The last event in Sequence C needs to end on a turning point that leads you into the next sequence. The protagonist has failed at his mini goal or achieved his mini goal. Either way it should lead to the next sequence.

Jerry Maguire has won Cushman as a client. He rejoices and sings as the radio is blasting. This event leads to the next sequence in the movie.

TO DO

ADD FIVE EVENTS TO YOUR CORKBOARD.

This is the third column. Is each scene cause and effect? Do the events lead to cause and effect? Does one thing cause the next thing to happen, or lead to the next thing? Do you have physical comedy in the story? Have you introduced your subplots?

On a third page, write the action/prose of what happens in your story.

● EXERCISE IN CONFLICT: THE AGITATOR

In a story, in a scene, you should always be looking for conflict. Remember — it don't come easy. Take a piece of a paper
and draw a line down the middle so you have two columns.

On the left side, title the column WHAT I DID TODAY. Now,
write down what you did today from the time you woke up to
the time you fell asleep. If you're reading this in the morning,
use yesterday.

It can be as simple as:
WOKE UP
EXERCISED
MADE BREAKFAST
TOOK BUS TO WORK
MET WITH BOSS ABOUT NEW PROJECT

Not the most exciting things in the world. Now, on the right
side — at the TOP — write BUT. Not BUTT. Just BUT.

Now we're going to generate conflict. Let's start moving
down the list. Be spontaneous. Be stream of consciousness.

WOKE UP *but* didn't know where I was from a long night of
drinking. Who is this woman in the bed with me?

EXERCISED *but* my exercise pants got caught on the
Stairmaster and ripped.

MADE BREAKFAST *but* my Mom called and I spilled milk
all over my only clean suit, which I needed for a job interview.

TOOK THE BUS TO WORK *but* it was robbed and suddenly
I was in the middle of a *Speed*-like chase.

MET WITH MY BOSS ABOUT A NEW PROJECT *but* the
project is about automating the company. If I do my job, I am
out of a job. As you develop your story, you are always looking to make things complicated.

CHAPTER EIGHT

COMIC SEQUENCE (D)

IT JUST KEEPS GETTING WORSE A.K.A.

HOW MUCH PAIN CAN BEN STILLER TAKE?

Your protagonist has tried and failed to solve his initial problem with the easiest possible solution — or he has started on the road of his journey only to have something unexpected happened. The guys can't find Doug in *The Hangover*. *Dave* is adjusting to life as President but realizes that the First Lady hates him. As Sequence D begins, your protagonist will make a second attempt to fix his problem.

PLAN B

Drunk ladies in the bar didn't take care of that chronic virginity problem, let's go to Plan B. You got the star football kid as a client, time to sell him at the NFL draft.

You and your hero need to know what Plan B is. What is the next course of action in your story? It's all about righting the wrong. All Shrek wants is to get the fairytale creatures out of his forest. Sequence C (Mad, Mad, Mad,

Mad World) was walking and being stuck with Donkey. Now, it's time to storm the castle.

Protagonists will either fail at Plan B, or it will lead to another, bigger complication. Hence: It just keeps getting worse. Mel in *Flirting with Disaster* journeys to San Diego only to find out he does not come from a very blonde, very athletically gifted family. He learns his father is in Minnesota. Time to go to Plan B! Minnesota!

INTIMACY THROUGH FAILURE

We want to see protagonists fail. Even if something good has happened to the protagonist, the good is not going to last long. It can't. If it does, the story will become uninteresting. You want to test the resolve of your main character. How much is she willing to put up with to get what she wants? Audiences tend to bond with characters that fail but try again. It appeals to the fighter in all of us. Also, we're glad it's not us to whom this failure is happening. But having characters struggle to achieve their goals keeps the outcome of the movie in doubt.

Greg is trying to impress his father-in-law in *Meet the Parents*. He messes up the dinner, knocks over the urn with his mother-in-law's ashes; he messes up the toilet. He will burn the wedding arch to the ground. He will break the nose of the bride. He will lose dad's cat and try to swap out a new one. The new one will destroy the wedding dress! That is all in Act Two. In Act Three, he will be arrested for saying the word, "bomb" on a plane.

Why do we like this guy? He can't do anything right! We bond with Greg because his desire is primal. He wants to impress. He loves Pam and wants to fit in. Of course, Jack, his father-in-law, is a worthy adversary. He is the toughest man in the world to please. Comic opposites. They battle through the entire movie. If Jack were a push-over, no movie. No failure. No intimacy with Greg.

FIVE EVENTS TO THE MIDPOINT

In this sequence, the next column of your screenplay, you will be adding *five new events*. The best part of the comic structure is that you need an idea of where you are going. Why? So you can get there.

No one leaves their house in the morning and just decides to walk to Los Angeles. They make a plan. They need to pack. Rent a van. Figure out a route. Know where they are going to stay. *Structure is your roadmap*. Yes, you will make side-trips to visit strange new places. Go there. Let your characters take you there. But then get them back on the road.

Just like with any trip, you have an idea *when you are half way there*. I want you to start thinking about the *midpoint* of your screenplay. The next five events in this sequence will end Act Two-A. It's like an act break. A curtain coming down in a theatrical show. Something is going to happen. When a big event is happening in the story put in some *anticipation scenes*.

ANTICIPATION AND REACTION SCENES

What makes stories real? The characters. You make a sci-fi comedy blockbuster like *Galaxy Quest*. Nothing feels real in that entire movie. Aliens. Spaceships. We know it's a movie — but the characters are so well drawn, so real that we are connected to them. So what makes the characters real? Scenes of emotion.

Humanize your characters by giving them scenes of *anticipation* and *reaction*. Show us how your characters are feeling about the events in the movie. Don't be talking about the past. Talk about the now.

Ted finally gets a date with Mary. Show a scene of anticipation. He is nervous. Getting dressed. He wants everything to go right. Of course, his best friend gives him some off-color advice about cleaning the pipes, so he does. The point is we have spent time with Ted as he *anticipates* going on his date.

Think of it like the fighter waiting for the big fight. In Sequence D (It Just Keeps Getting Worse) of *Jerry Maguire*, Jerry is heading for the NFL draft. Dorothy and Ray drive him to the airport. They talk about the draft, where he is staying, what he will be doing. Everyone is getting amped up for the moment. Because the upcoming event is big in the protagonist's eyes, it's big in ours.

Shrek sees the castle. It's at the end of a long bridge and it looks very foreboding. Donkey is scared. Yes, it's getting worse.

REACTION SCENES

Reaction scenes are what happens after something happens! Don't be afraid to have your characters talk about what just happened! Immediately after Greg's horrible prayer at the family dinner in *Meet the Parents,* we see Greg and Pam reacting to what happened. Immediately after the horses die by running off a cliff in *City Slickers,* we see Mitch eulogizing the horses. Reaction!

RAMPING UP

The protagonist is gearing toward a big emotional shift. He doesn't know it yet, but you do. Something is going to happen at the midpoint of the movie, which will create an *emotional shift* in your protagonist. They have been fighting to restore things to status quo since the story began; or, they have been striving for a goal they think they want, but at the midpoint of the story something will happen to them that is going to get them on the path to becoming whole, and repairing whatever is really wrong with them emotionally, inside.

If there's going to be an emotional shift, an emotional turning point, I think the events leading up to that need to be of heightened, sustained drama. Yes, I said drama in a comedy. Never forget that even though you are writing it for laughs, it is life or death for the characters.

BACKWARD FROM THE MIDPOINT

I often tell my students to work backward here. Think about what happens at the midpoint of your story, or what should happen, and put your protagonist through hell getting there.

The midpoint. What exactly is it?

The half-way mark of a movie. It is almost like another act break. If there were an intermission in a movie, it would be at the midpoint. Remember, the beginning of Act Two was the fun and games. Not much had to happen except that you had to deliver on the promise of the premise, that is you had some fun with your protagonist in an unexpected situation; you had some jokes, as with the guys in *Wedding Crashers* pretending to be someone else in order to win over girls at weddings.

So far in the second act, although the situation was a new mad, mad, mad, mad world, your protagonist really has no interest in changing her ways. She knows there is a problem in her life but damn if she knows what it is. Remember, it's all about characters.

THE MIDPOINT HINTS AT THE ENDING

None of these characters has begun to change knowingly. The first big transformation occurs at the *midpoint* of the script. Now here's a little clue: Sometimes the midpoint of the movie points to the ending of the movie. It is the first hint of how the story is going to end. It's the big emotional plant for the end.

Here are some examples:

There's Something About Mary
Midpoint: Ted finally sees Mary again in Florida. It's the first time they are together in the movie since the opening.
End of the movie: Ted and Mary are together.

Forgetting Sarah Marshall
Midpoint: Peter (Jason Segal) is on a date with Rachel (Mila Kunis.) He sings his *Dracula* song for a show that he hasn't been able to finish.
End of the movie: Peter is performing his *Dracula* puppet show that he's finally finished and Mila Kunis is in the audience and they are finally together.

The 40-Year-Old Virgin
Midpoint: Andy (Steve Carell) asks Trish (Catherine Keener) out for the first time.
End of the movie: Andy and Trish get married. Andy gets laid for the first time.

Jerry Maguire
Midpoint: Jerry loses his client; breaks up with Avery.
End of the movie: Jerry is with Dorothy.

The common element is that a major event happens at the *midpoint* and more times than not there is a ramping up toward that event. Think back on scenes that lead up to those midpoints just discussed. There are some pretty sustained sequences. There's a lot of dramatic weight loaded into those scenes. This goal is going to be the bulk of the next sequence of your scriptment — *It just keeps getting worse.*

In *Forgetting Sarah Marshall,* Peter cannot get over Sarah Marshall even though he has been hanging out with her. There is a fight on the beach.

In *There's Something About Mary,* Ted goes through hell to get to Mary in Florida. From picking up a crazy hitchhiker, the rest stop incident, cross-talk with police, and getting beaten up during interrogation.

It just keeps getting worse might consist of a sustained sequence leading up to the major event of the midpoint, which is why it is so important to know what is happening at the midpoint.

In *Almost Famous,* Russell the rocker, is out of control at a party in a small town. The teenage journalist, William, is with him every step of the way, trying to save him from himself. After a long night of drinking and diving off a roof, the rocker is reunited on the tour. William returns to the bus and is told by Penny that he is "home." William is finding out who he is, where he belongs.

IMPORTANCE OF LOCATION

Take a moment to think about where the midpoint of the story takes place. Will a location add to the conflict? A destination that the protagonist has been heading toward? The NFL Draft serves as a wonderful arena for *Jerry Maguire.* Jerry attends the draft with great expectations (anticipation scenes); his enemies are there. The audience is wondering — what is going to happen? Will Jerry be able to keep his client? It doesn't happen in an office. It happens in his arena. Shrek finds Fiona in a castle. He rescues her. It's not in the middle of the forest.

TO DO:

ADD FIVE MORE CARDS/EVENTS

Write out the prose on your fourth sheet of paper.

SEQUENCE CHEAT SHEET

- Establish your protagonist's sequence goal early in the sequence.
- Make the approach a sustained approach.
- Make sure the midpoint of the movie points/hints at the ending of the story.
- Does the structure of the sequence have a beginning, middle, and an end?
- Does something unexpected happen?
- Do I have action and reaction scenes?

CHAPTER NINE

COMIC SEQUENCE (E)

L'OVE IS IN THE AIR

A.K.A. WHY ANDY CHOOSES L'OVE

OVER SEX

By the time you have reached the midpoint, an extensive set of questions and characters has been introduced. You have been working at this frenetic pace. The story is building and building, and then something odd happens.

The story slows down. It's like someone takes the foot off the gas. And it happens in this next comic sequence, Love Is In the Air. Remember we talked about hilarity and heart?

It's time for the heart.

It's where the heart of your comedy is going to emerge. It's where you are going to develop the theme.

This section is where you really get a chance to develop the theme — and while doing that your protagonist is making very little progress toward the actual goal.

It's dramatic.

In *Witness* (not a comedy blockbuster, but bear with me), halfway through the movie John Book decides to stay hidden. He has learned it is not safe. The development section moves in a direction that suggests John Book might fit into the Amish community through his love for Rachel, denouncing his violent profession. The development section usually ends at the point where all the premises regarding the goals and the lines of action have been introduced.

In this part John Book is not doing anything to stop the crooked cops. This section is where he is *building a barn*. It has nothing to do with the plot of the movie but has everything to do with *what the movie is all about!*

So let's take a moment and look at *comedy and drama*. On a side note, your characters don't think they are in a comedy — they think they are in a life-or-death struggle. For instance, take *Old School,* Frank the Tank gets married, separates from his wife, watches an old man die, gets divorced. What part of that is funny? It's the old adage — it's funny because it happened to him and not you.

So just as we've been building the scriptment by identifying specific comedic beats, we will now do that with this section. Love In the Air matures the screenplay. It makes it about something.

We'll hit five events for Sequence E: Love is in the Air.

So the first thing we need to do is fill in:

REACTION TO THE MIDPOINT

The *midpoint* is a major event. Something substantial has just happened to your protagonist. When something major happens in your life, you react. The next event is the *reaction to the midpoint.* We want to talk about what is going on. The characters and the audience need to react to what is going on around them. Give them a chance to breathe.

At the midpoint of *Jerry Maguire,* Jerry has lost it all. He has lost his star client; he has been punched out by his girlfriend. There is a great beat where Rod Tidwell (Cuba Gooding) yells, "You're loving me now." The reaction occurs on the airplane. Jerry is drowning his sorrows talking about what just happened. Rod reminds him of the goal — as he still needs a contract. He also tells Jerry he believes in him even though no one else does.

MAJOR CHARACTER SHIFT

Remember: The most important thing in a story is how the character will transform; how they will change. It's really starting to be pronounced at this point in the story. The character shift is occurring.

That was the midpoint — a new event, incident, or piece of information that is the worst thing that can happen to the character so far.

You are watching *Forgetting Sarah Marshall* the first time. Peter has performed his *Dracula* musical at the middle in a bar. Rachel loved it. She encourages him to keep writing it. We're enjoying the comedy and the romance. We don't notice that Peter is on his first step to recovery.

In *The 40-Year-Old Virgin*, Andy just wants to get laid. But then something happens around the midpoint. This man who is really a boy begins to grow up. He begins to fall in love, which is the worst thing for him in terms of his goal to get laid.

In *Wedding Crashers,* John asks Jeremy for more time. He is falling in love and needs to stay. Jeremy will stay. On a side note: *Wedding Crashers* is a romantic comedy between the two guys. They are together, at the end of the second act they break up, and they get back together at the end at a wedding.

In *Jerry Maguire*, Jerry goes over to Dorothy's. He is drunk. He is demonstrating very inappropriate behavior. The next day he feels terrible and apologizes. He and Dorothy agree nothing should happen, so the next thing they do is go to dinner — and Jerry begins to *fall in love.*

Did you catch that? He begins to *fall in love.*

At the midpoint of *There's Something About Mary,* Ted finds Mary. That night they go on a date and then we see a montage. A series of shots as Ted and Mary... *fall in love.*

Are you seeing a pattern here? This pattern is why we call this section Love is in the Air. It usually is. Your protagonist's life is changing. It's not going to be easy. There are many complications to work through.

DEVELOP THE THEME

While all this love stuff is happening, this sequence gives you some room to develop the theme; it's a place to express what the movie is really about. It's the slower part of the symphony. This section draws upon the reasons you wanted to write the movie. This change is what the story is really all about.

This movie is still a comedy. So how do you balance that out with this whole heart thing here? Things appear to be going well for your hero — but never forget to keep knocking them down. We want to see how our heroes pick themselves up when things don't go well. We're looking for that moment where we feel really bad for what is happening to them.

In *There's Something About Mary,* this point is where the romance really kicks in. Ted is told that he needs to prepare for his date. His best friend, Dom (Chris Eliott), warns him about going out with a loaded gun. He encourages Ted to masturbate. Ted follows the advice and, as there is a knock on the door, he can't find his load. We see that it's hanging from his ear. The audience howls, cringes. We're thinking "Oh no! That poor guy." And then, the Farrelly Brothers, in an inspired moment, have Mary (Cameron Diaz) mistake the load for hair gel. She takes some. Now the audience is really howling. We like Mary — we feel her mistake. And then one more time — the Farrelly Brothers cut to the bar where Mary's hair is sticking straight up into the air.

Jerry Maguire has no idea how to pursue Dorothy. He does it all wrong at first. Our protagonists become more intimate as they fail. You know why? Because we fail. We want to see people who are like us. We like people who take it on the chin, get up, and try again.

UPPING THE STAKES

Love helps the story in two ways. One, it slows down the story and makes it more real. It grounds the movie. It balances the hilarity and the heart. It also UPS THE STAKES in the movie. Someone might get hurt. Real emotions are involved.

Also, DECEPTION may be involved; Deceiving someone you now love makes it worse. As discussed, deception is a device that has been used often and effectively in comedy. In *The 40-Year-Old Virgin,* Andy's not telling Trish (Catherine Keener) that he is a virgin is a deception; in *There's Something About Mary,* Ted's not telling Mary that he is basically stalking her is a comedy!

These lies will be exposed and the hero will have to come clean. You want to hold off on this moment for as long as possible. If the truth comes out too soon, it will not have as much weight.

At the opening of *Tootsie,* Michael Dorsey is an egotistical actor who is pretty much out for himself. He has friends, so we know he has some good qualities. In the guise of Dorothy Michaels, Michael begins exhibiting qualities he has never had before. He is a mentor, a friend. He cares about other people. He has fallen in love with Julie! The *emotional stakes* have been raised. More people are involved, so there are more feelings. *Tootsie* will continue to increase the emotional stakes as it nears the end of Act Two. Also, *the dramatic stakes* have increased. Dorothy Michaels now plays the most popular television soap opera character.

In *School of Rock,* Dewey has helped the kids gain confidence. What started as a ruse has now turned serious. He has unwittingly become a good teacher. Remember, the midpoint hints at the ending. We worry about what is going to happen when the school finds out who he really is.

In *Jerry Maguire,* Jerry and Dorothy begin a relationship. Her son, Ray, loves Jerry. He is the father the boy never had. Now what? What is going to happen there? Meanwhile, Rod is going to have a baby! He still needs that contract from the Arizona Cardinals!

But the characters are not worried about that right now — for a moment, all is good in the world. Montage fills the screen. Shrek bounces through the forest with Fiona. Ted is wooing Mary. Life is good.

Sometimes they are not even worried about what their original goal was. They are lost in the moment.

THE JOLT

The protagonist is not going toward her ultimate goal in this Comic Sequence. But at the end *something* jolts the protagonist back into the main action of the story.

Jerry and Dorothy are in love. All is going well when they get a contract offer for Rod Tidwell. (This event jolts us back to the main story, which is "Will Jerry make it on his own as an agent?") We had forgotten about it.

In *Forgetting Sarah Marshall*, all has been going well for Peter. He has been falling in love with Rachel (Mila Kunis) when there is a long dinner and Sarah starts wondering if she made a mistake. No, the audience shouts! You're supposed to be forgetting her. We like this new girl! Don't go back with her!

TO DO

Take a look at comedy blockbusters you admire. Go to the midpoint. What happens right after the midpoint for the next ten to thirteen minutes? You might be surprised to see how it is not as funny as what came before or what is to come after.

ADD FIVE MORE EVENTS/CARDS TO YOUR BOARD

Concentrate on developing the theme. What is your unique point of view of the world? About love?

- Write up the prose on your fifth piece of paper.
- Is there a character shift?
- Have you reacted to the midpoint?
- Is the theme developed?
- Is love in the air?
- Have you upped the stakes?
- Did you jolt the characters back to reality?

● COMIC EXERCISE: THE SOUNDTRACK

A few years ago a friend of mine wrote about book about how music can "tune your brain." She posited that when you hear feel-good music, you start to feel good. When you exercise to the same music, your body knows it's time to exercise. When you put on "Bolero," you start thinking of the movie *10*.

I used to associate writing different projects with different music. One summer all I listened to was David Gray as I finished a production polish. I cannot listen to any of his *White Ladder* album without thinking of that project.

Comedy and music go hand in hand. Soundtracks have pop songs and musical cues. Think about ten songs that are representative of the movie you are writing. Can you imagine them playing over some of the scenes you already have in your head? The credits?

Go ahead and make that playlist on whatever musical player you have. For the next week, you can only listen to those songs, or those artists, when you are writing your comedy blockbuster.

CHAPTER TEN

COMIC

SEQUENCE (F)

WHAT WAS I THINKING?

A.K.A. YES, I'M A LIAR BUT...

It seems like a lifetime ago that the fool set off on a journey. They have lied, deceived, not told the whole truth, lived in drag, lied to themselves, struggled with who they are and who they will become. Ben in *Knocked Up* is a slacker stoner, but he is also going to be a father. Your fool has also been on the road to maturity. He is getting close, but he is not there yet.

We are entering the last thirteen to fifteen minutes of the second act of a screenplay. The stakes have been increased. The hero has more to lose than when the journey began. Harry loves Sally. New York City needs the Ghostbusters.

A FINAL PUSH

The protagonist is going to make that final push to achieve the goal. They are going to do anything they can. What they need to do to achieve that goal is what provides the objective for this sequence.

All sequences have a mini-objective, which is achieved or not achieved. Or it's a road movie moving from place to place. Where are your characters now?

In *Flirting with Disaster,* Mel (Ben Stiller) has been looking for his birth parents. He knows how to find them. Richard and Mary (Alan Alda and Lilly Tomlin) are living in Arizona. He visits. It looks great! He finally has made it.

In the classic *Animal House,* the guys from Delta House decide to have a final bash. The classic toga party! This entire sequence is a set piece. Remember: A set piece is an extended sequence of comedic madness that usually takes place in one enclosed location. This scene is Delta House's final push toward debauchery.

GOOD TIMES NEVER LAST

The second act is going to have a balance of good times/ bad times. We have to give the protagonist a little hope. This isn't a comedy based on the Book of Job. Your main character is a fool (on the inside or on the outside). So when good times are happening for him — he should never get too comfortable. The audience knows this good time isn't going to last. But we hope it will.

Emotionally, you want to give the audience and your character a glimpse of what a happy life can look like. It's Shrek in love with Fiona. It's Ted in love with Mary. It's the sequence in *Tootsie* where Michael (dressed as Dorothy Michaels) realizes he is in love with Julie. He goes to her farm and visits her Dad (Les). It's the perfect family moment. Cooking dinner. Singing songs. Life can be good for Michael — except for the fact that he is in drag! And the father of the woman Michael's in love with has fallen in love with him! He is a fool!

It's the sequence in *Dave* when Dave is saving the country, changing policy, and falling in love with the First Lady. There's only one problem, Dave is not the real President!

In this sequence, our fools are forgetting who they are and what they did to get there. All Greg wanted in *Meet the Parents* was to impress his future father-in-law, Jack. Now at the dinner, the night before the wedding, Jack has let Greg into his circle of trust! It's all great — except for the fact that Greg spray-painted a cat to get back into the circle!

These good times are never going to last.

EXPOSE THE CHARACTER'S WEAKNESS

During the course of the story — and I've noticed it takes place a lot before the end of the second act — you might want to expose the character's weakness. What is the character's weakness? Remember Superman? He had kryptonite. What is your hero's weakness? What is she vulnerable to?

We talked about the ghost/inner wound in character work. What haunts the hero? Sometimes the protagonist will talk about it. It's the moment where the fool who has been lying almost tells the truth. He or she will almost confess — but doesn't.

In *There's Something About Mary*, Mary opens up about the other guy in her life. It will turn out to be Brett Favre. Mary talks about how Brett lied to her about Warren and how he broke her heart. She has a no-lying rule. She tells this to Ted — the ultimate stalker/liar!

In *Wedding Crashers,* John (Owen Wilson) has fallen in love with Claire (Rachel McAdams). They have many things in common. He loves her. She probably loves him. He thinks it's a good idea to tell her that he is completely full of shit. Of course, this moment is interrupted.

In *Shrek,* Shrek overhears Fiona talking about her curse. She has revealed to Donkey that she is really an ogre. Shrek doesn't hear everything she says. He gets confused and thinks she is talking about what a hideous creature he is. Our favorite ogre now has a moment of self-hatred. He retreats and reverts to his old angry self.

The Calm Before the Storm

Just before the end of Act Two there's sometimes a calming moment. The end of Act Two is going to be pretty eventful for the protagonist. And now — just before things get crazy at the end of Act Two — there might be a moment of calm. Sometimes The Calm Before the Storm and Expose the Character Weakness blend....

In *Bull Durham,* Annie (Susan Sarandon) has fallen in love with Crash (Kevin Costner), breaking her rule. All is calm. All is good.

End of Act Two: Bad Things Happen

At the end of the first act, protagonists want to restore the status quo. Jerry Maguire just wants his job back. Shrek wants the fairytale creatures out of his forest. They feel they have lost what is important to them. But by the end of this sequence, they have lost even more.

In the beginning of *Groundhog Day,* all Phil wants to do is get out of Punxsutawney. He is thinking of taking a job in Los Angeles. By the end of the second act, by the end of this sequence, Phil realizes he is going to lose the woman he now loves.

They have gone after the inappropriate goal thinking it was a good idea — and hey, it seemed like a good idea at the time — but now, as we near the end of Act Two, the fool has a realization: simply put — he shouts at the sky and wonders *what was I thinking?*

They can't believe they have been foolish enough to love, to lie. They foolishly think they were happy before they found love.

The end of Act Two is the biggest *OH NO!* moment in the script. One way to look at it is *bad things really happen.* Your protagonist's life has fallen apart even more than it did before. Now things are really terrible. Thoughts are racing through his mind. "How did I get myself into this?" "What was I thinking?!?!"

It's all about *emotional investment.* Your protagonist has invested emotionally in the second act. They care about things in a different way. Now, they stand to lose even more than they ever had.

In *Wedding Crashers,* John will lose the woman he loves because he lied. At the end of the second act, the lie is exposed! The deception is revealed. What was I thinking??! This leads to a *break-up.* Remember — romance is involved here. If the relationship looks like it has a chance, it doesn't any more.

Andy loses the girl in *The 40-Year-Old Virgin.* Ben and Allison break up in *Knocked Up.*

In *Flirting with Disaster,* Mel Coplin (Ben Stiller) is given LSD by his half-brother who hates him! What was I thinking?!?!

In *Bull Durham,* Crash is traded. And he is in love with Annie.

In *Animal House*, it's all over for Delta House.

Another way to think about the end of Act Two: It's the event where the protagonist is now as far away as possible from achieving what her heart desires.

In a multiprotagonist story like *Little Miss Sunshine*, bad things happen at this point to all of our characters — Richard feels like a failure now that his book deal is dead; Dwayne learns that he can't get into the air force; Sheryl is worried that her marriage and family are coming apart.

It's falling apart for all the characters! Remember, they all thought they were the hero of the movie.

OTHER WAYS TO END ACT TWO

It doesn't always have to be the big *OH NO!* moment. There are other ways to end the second act of your comedy blockbuster.

THE EDGE OF BATTLE

In action comedies, the end of the second act might bring the protagonist to the edge of battle. In *Ghostbusters* and *Men In Black,* the final battle is about to begin. The ghosts are all over New York. The Ghostbusters are in jail and Zuul, the demi-god, is about to arrive and destroy the world. In *Men in Black,* the Bugs are about to destroy the earth unless they get what they want.

A NEW GOAL

Sometimes the original goal that drove the comic engine is replaced at the end of the second act. The protagonist might have achieved what he wanted — but along the way (Act Two) he realized that he wanted something more. Here's a hint: It's usually love.

Shrek achieved his goal. He brought Fiona to the King. The fairytale creatures are gone from his swamp. Life is good. He got what he wanted. But it's not what he needed. He didn't know what he needed until he was on this comic journey.

At the end of the second act of *Tootsie,* Dorothy's contract has been renewed. He just wanted work. He now has work. He has money. He is famous. But now he wants Julie.

PURPOSES OF THE END OF ACT TWO

The end of the second act changes the action around, moving the story into Act Three. In some ways the end of the second act accomplishes the same thing as the first turning point: It turns the action around in a new direction. It raises the dramatic question again, and makes us wonder about the answer. It raises the stakes. And it pushes the story into the next and final act.

TO DO

Write the sixth page of your treatment. Think of it as a beginning, middle, and end. At the end of the second act is your protagonist at the end of her emotional rope? Have they lost the new thing they now love?

ADD FIVE MORE EVENTS/CARDS TO YOU BOARD

CHAPTER ELEVEN

ACT THREE

COMIC SEQUENCE (G)

TIME TO GROW UP A.K.A. WHY
ARE ASHTON AND NATALIE SO
SAD EVEN THOUGH THEY SAID
NO STRINGS ATTACHED?

THOUGHTS ABOUT ACT THREE

So now we get into Act Three. As the screenplay for *Terminator 2* by James Cameron and William Wisher reads: "OKAY, BUCKLE YOUR SEATBELTS, HERE IT COMES."

You have reached the point where the story can carry itself.

You will find the writing gets faster and faster here and you rush toward the finish, eagerly writing down the remaining beats, which is why, once again, we pull back a little and make sure it works in the scriptment.

Act Three is NOT an afterthought. It's roughly the same length as Act One and Act Two-A or Act Two-B. Though the "story time" is accelerated, the page length remains the same.

Let's keep some things in mind. Act Three is all about heading toward the resolution. Everything up to this point pays off. This act is where your *main character* undergoes *the final transformation.*

You want to think of your Act Three in terms of your main character. This act is where he is going to be tested the most. He has gone on the fool's journey and now will shed his old skin and become someone new.

You are approaching the event that confronts the protagonist; when, faced with the most powerful forces of antagonism in his life, he must now make a decision.

You are answering the dramatic question: What is going to happen? All movies ask a question. Time to answer it.

Will Ben get Mary?

Will Harry and Sally be together? And, thematically, which one of them is right? Can men and women be friends and not want to sleep with each other?

Will Delta House get revenge?

Will the guys in *Old School* keep the frat house?

Will the guys from *The Hangover* find Doug?

It all leads up to these moments — where the emotions kick in.

If you have a true end to your story, this part is easy. You will also notice that your writing pace will quicken here. You are rushing to the finish. But before you begin, let's deconstruct Act Three.

So What Is Act Three?

So what is Act Three? In his book *The Art of Dramatic Writing*, Lajos Egri states that, "Act three is when decisive change one way or another unfolds."

Everything leading up to the *climax* of the movie has been building toward some sort of *change*.

You want to blow them away. Give them something they want but don't expect. I have noticed there are different types of Act Threes.

Different Types of Act Threes

There is the *action* or *physical act three*. The second act ends. The protagonist is going to take on physical action. In this Act Three you have chase scenes and big battles. Big set pieces. The last act of *Animal House* is built around the big parade. The last act of *Old School* is the series of tests to validate the fraternity. *Knocked Up* ends with the birth. *Father of the Bride* ends with the wedding. *Four Weddings and a Funeral* is structured around four weddings and a funeral. In the last act, we get to the wedding: that of Charlie, our protagonist.

There is the *journey act three*. The last leg of the journey. Arriving at the destination. In *Vacation* the Griswald family has wanted to get to Wally World. In Act Three, they get there. In *Due Date*, Peter is finally nearing home and might get to see the birth of his baby.

And then there is the *talking act three*. This is the stuff dramas are made of. Think of how movies like *The Big Chill* or *Broadcast News* end. Huge emotional lettings.

What Else Should Happen In My Act Three?

LOOSE ENDS — Remember those subplots and all those other characters who thought they were the lead in the movie? They need endings, too. In the third act all of those separate story lines will converge and get wrapped up. Now, there's always someone who says they don't want to do that — that they hate movies that end with everything tied in a bow. You know what people hate more? Investing time in a character that disappears in the movie. Hey, what happened to that cousin of hers who was going to have that operation? If subplots do not come to some sort of conclusion, the audience feels like it has been a waste of time.

TICKING CLOCK — Another device used in the last act is the ticking clock. (If it hasn't shown up already, that is). By the final act, the hero is running out of time or a certain event is going to take place at an appointed time. You want to give the third act a sense of immediacy. Someone has to do X before Y happens.

Let's look at some examples of a ticking clock last act:

Ben has to find Elaine before she gets married. (*The Graduate*).

John has to become friends again with Jeremy before he gets married. (*Wedding Crashers*).

What the wedding does is give the last act and the movie an *endpoint* — a reference point. We know it's going to end, but we don't know how. The ticking clock devices give the protagonist the sense that he is running out of time and might not make it. These devices also help set up the *time and place* of the final battle.

Act Three is jam-packed with turns, reveals, and character growth. Act Three has more in it than any other act. As Arthur says to Hobson, "When we last left Hamlet, he was in big trouble." Think about where your protagonist was at the end of the second act. Some event happened to her or she knows she was on the verge of a final battle, or in the middle of a crisis. Throughout this book, I have stressed that what makes actors want to play the parts and what makes the difference between a great character and a good character are the moments of humanity. To me these are the moments where the protagonist acts as we would react — or, as we wish we would react.

When something goes wrong in life, and things don't work out the way you planned, there might be a moment where you dwell on it; commiserate with a friend. I've seen this in scripts. It's called...

SINGING THE BLUES

Something major has happened to the main character and now he is feeling pretty bad. People don't mind watching other people suffer and reflect and mourn and sing the blues. We are learning. We go to the movies to learn. To learn to love. To deal. To live. They are the myths. We want to see how people react to all that is going on around them. *Show me.* Have your characters feel pain. We can feel badly for them. The audience has earned it.

Once again, the pacing of the screenplay slows down as the third act begins.

Here are three examples:

At the end of the second act of *Wedding Crashers*, John has lost Claire. He is despondent and we see exactly how despondent he is. He looks like a mess. His apartment is a mess.

In *Knocked Up*, Ben Stone has broken up with Allison. She misses him. He misses her. Neither is going to say it.

In *Tootsie*, Michael learns his contract has been renewed and he is stuck in the contract; Julie isn't talking to him. We see him lamenting to his agent — you have to get me out of this. He feels trapped. Remember: It's okay to move events around within the sequence. In the last act of *Tootsie*, closer to the ending, we also see Michael walking alone through Central Park. He is lost. He feels horrible. So what does he do? He pushes a mime. It's a great comedy button at the end of your scene.

In *No Strings Attached*, Emma and Adam have broken up. Their sex-buddies thing has failed as they (gulp) have fallen in love. They feel awful…

WHO AM I?

At this point in the story, on an emotionally thematic level the protagonist is being ripped into two people. He is at war with himself. Is he the "he" he was before? Or, is he going to become this new better person? Just as there was the "What the hell was I thinking?" moment earlier where the character was filled with self-doubt, we see another moment of indecision, or even retreat. As mentioned there is the ticking clock and time is running out for them. They don't know what to do and that is why sometimes there's…

HELP FROM THE MENTOR

Donkey coming to visit Shrek in the swamp; Freddie in *Splash* telling Allen, "Who cares that she is a mermaid." It's okay to have that friend/mentor/sidekick be critical of the protagonist. It doesn't make the protagonist weak — it makes him human. You want the best friend to actually *be* the best friend and offer some sage advice; or, to kick your character in the butt and get him moving again.

Jeremy is trying to help John in *Wedding Crashers* but Jeremy (Owen Wilson) isn't listening. Instead, he seeks advice from a different kind of mentor, Chazz (Will Ferrell). Jeremy starts attending funerals.

In *Little Miss Sunshine*, the Hoover family members become each other's mentors. They start picking each other up. Nothing plays better than when little Olive consoles her brother on the side of the road.

THE LAST GREAT DECISION

The character faces a crisis. What to do? What am I going to do now? They have loved. And they have lost. They have tried something new — and it has failed. They have only made things worse in their life. What are they going to do now?

Your fool has a moment here where she faces the choice: Be the fool forever or finally change. Grow up. Mature. This sequence is called *Time to Grow Up* for a reason. That growth is what needs to happen to spin the story into the final sequence, to send it rocking to the conclusion.

Your fool is going to make that *last great decision*. They realize they cannot go on living the way they were living before. Like a snake shedding its skin, they are going to change their skin now. It's time.

Ben in *Knocked Up* decides it's to grow up. Get a job. Get that crib. Start working for the baby. We see him reading a baby book.

Ben in *The Graduate* decides he is going to marry Elaine. How? He's not sure. But he knows — it's time.

The Hoover family will not be deterred. They have come this far and are going to make it to the Little Miss Sunshine pageant.

This is the moment of change. And the protagonist, charged with this newly found persona and usually charged with love — goes into those final fifteen minutes of the movie ready for battle. Leading toward the resolution...

TO DO:

Add five more events to your next column ending with the *Last Great Decision.*

Write one more page to your treatment.

CHAPTER TWELVE

COMIC SEQUENCE (H)

THE NEW ME A.K.A. WHY BEN STILLER,

JIM CARREY, HUGH GRANT, NATALIE PORTMAN

ARE RUNNING AT THE END OF THE MOVIE

It's time for the big ending. This denouement is what people have paid for. This resolution is what they want to see. Explosions. Confrontations. Hijinks should ensue! Secrets should be revealed!

The movie is called *Little Miss Sunshine*. We have heard all about the Little Miss Sunshine contest. It's time to get there.

The movie is called *Wedding Crashers*. Someone should be crashing a wedding at the end.

Here are some of the events that tend to take place in the last thirteen to fifteen minutes of a comedy:

THE BATTLE

There's the battle. The confrontation. The climax. Because of that "SOMETHING HAPPENS" moment way back on page thirteen of your script, the end of your first column, the bottom of your page — The Battle had to happen. The audience has been waiting for it. Expecting it. And if you don't deliver it — they are going to hate you.

The writer has been telling the audience the whole time: Expect a happy ending. It is a comedy. But how we get there is the fun. They might get it — but the heroes have to earn it. Don't make it easy.

In *Tootsie*, the battle is that famous last scene where Michael reveals himself to be a man on the live taping of the soap opera. Key words here: *live taping*. The idea was planted earlier in the script that they occasionally do a live taping.

In *City Slickers*, "the battle" is the final push to drive the cattle home. It's raining and they have to cross a river. One of the most important thoughts you can give your ending is — *Where does it take place?* This is called...

CONVERGENCE

...All the forces that have been gathering are heading for a collision course. But where is it going to take place? What is the best arena for the battle? What location have we seen that we can use again? Or, what location have we been heading toward?

Tootsie's battle has to take place on the soap stage. Anything else would not feel right. In *Jerry Maguire*, it's the football game — the big one at the end. On national television. *Wedding Crashes, Shrek, Four Weddings and a Funeral* all end in a church.

When Harry Met Sally ends on New Year's Eve. Earlier in the screenplay, the characters talked about what to do if they don't have dates for the next New Year's Eve. Now it *is* that next New Year's Eve. A significant location has been set up in the story.

A convergence of characters should also be occurring. Bring everyone back to the party. In *Flirting With Disaster,* it's a romp around the desert and the house. But not just any house; it's the home of Ben Stiller's real birth parents.

Any character of significance should be in the ending of your movie.

To not have them all here would like be like forgetting to invite a close family member to a wedding.

SACRIFICE

In the last act sometimes you will see a sacrifice — not of a lamb but of one person for the greater good.

In *There's Something About Mary,* Ted loves Mary. He knows he has messed up and he will never be with her. But that doesn't stop him from making a sacrifice. He does the thing that causes him the most pain in life — he brings Brett Favre to Mary. He wants her to be happy.

RESURRECTION

Another event that occurs in the final battle is a resurrection. We want life-changing, life-affirming experiences. Resurrection occurs through death — but here we're speaking metaphorically. For a character to be reborn sometimes, she needs to experience death — death of a relationship, physical death, emotional death.

How can you show this? A relationship ends and then is revived. Mitch dives into the water in *City Slickers* to save

Norman the Cow. He is drowning. He hits his head on a rock. He almost dies. He experiences death.

In *Jerry Maguire,* Rod Tidwill is knocked out on national television during a football game. His wife is home watching. Jerry is there. Rod is down. The football cradled in his arms. Then he opens his eyes, leaps up. Full of life — soaking in the adoration of the fans who now love him.

In a romance or romantic comedy, the resurrection can be learning to love again. The renewal of the relationship. Harry and Sally's love is resurrected on New Year's Eve.

EPIPHANY

Every meeting in Hollywood is all about this moment. The studio exec's favorite question is — *What is his/her epiphany?*

What does this mean? It was done brilliantly in *The Simpsons Movie,* as we got to see Homer wonder what an epiphany was and experience it in front of us. If you were sitting in a Los Angeles theater watching that movie, the people laughing the loudest were the writers.

What does it mean? According to dictionary.com, an epiphany is (1) an unusually sudden manifestation or perception of the essential nature or meaning of something; (2) an intuitive grasp of reality through something (as an event) usually simple and striking; (3) an illuminating discovery or a revealing scene or moment.

It's about what the hero has learned — and what the audience has learned.

In *When Harry Met Sally,* we see Harry walking around New York. It's New Year's Eve. He is alone. Sally is at the party. Harry looks up at the Washington Square Park arch. It's the same place where he first dropped off Sally after they drove to New York together years ago. Now images flood his mind: Quick shots of the good times together. Harry Connick, Jr. starts crooning "It Had To Be You." Harry gets it! He knows what he wants.

(And yes, that is all in the script. The writer wrote it).

In *Jerry Maguire*, Rod Tidwell has had this amazing game on national television. Jerry waits for him in the hallway outside the locker room. People are saying hello to him again. Bob Sugar is there with his client. Out comes Rod and hugs Jerry. People admire their relationship; other players are interested. Rod finally gets the attention that he always wanted. Reporters and cameramen are in his face. Rod picks up the phone. It's his wife. In the middle of all this, all Rod cares about is saying, "I love you" to his wife. Jerry watches it. He can stay at the party and be at the top of his game. But he has that epiphany. That moment where it all makes sense. Jerry has learned that nothing is as important to him as when you have someone who loves you.

THE FINAL RACE

Sometimes — and especially in comedies — there's the race or the chase. You've seen it. Getting to the airport. Racing to the train. Ben running to the wedding. In *When Harry Met Sally,* Harry is running across the city. In *Liar, Liar* Fletcher is chasing the plane. Broad. Funny.

In *Knocked Up,* Ben is racing to get to the hospital before his baby is born. Will he get there in time?

And finally — and this does have to come at the end — the last beat is...

THE NEW ME

The fool is dead. They have learned so much about themselves on this journey. They are a polar opposite of who they were when we first met them. All those problems they had have been solved. It is a comedy. They are not alone in the world anymore.

How do you visualize this? It's show-and-tell time.

In *When Harry Met Sally,* Harry says it on New Year's Eve. He loves her. In *Old School,* Mitch gets the girl. He is mature. The Ghostbusters are the heroes! They are recognized and appreciated for who they are. They are no longer the joke of the community.

In *Animal House*, subtitles tell us what happens to the characters after college.

The fool stands there, having completed his or her journey — a new person. A better person.

Mel in *Flirting With Disaster* is at peace knowing who his parents are — they are the people who adopted him, raised him.

Richard Hoover in *Little Miss Sunshine* has danced on stage with his daughter and his crazy family. He is a much better person and in a much better place than he was when the movie began.

Ben Stone in *Knocked Up* has a job. He is a family man. Talk about sacrifice! But he is happy.

Now, the last thing you need to do before you write THE END....

TAKE A BREATH AT THE END

The resolution allows for a breath. It allows for the emotional impact to settle in, instead of just slamming the credits in the audience's face. The resolution is the cinematic equivalent of the theater's slow curtain. It's the scene at the end of *Jerry*

Maguire where Jerry, Ray, and Dorothy are walking though the park and Ray throws a ball. Shrek dancing in the swamp.

A Word About Satisfying Endings

A satisfying ending does not mean a happy ending. It means an ending that satisfies everything that came before it.

A word about happy endings: I like them. I'm a pretty positive person. I love the movies and want the hero to get the girl and the bad guy to die. I'm a simple man with simple needs. So is the movie-going audience.

Little Miss Sunshine was a movie with a very off-beat, satisfying happy ending. Olive does not win. But the Hoovers have won.

Ben runs off with Elaine in *The Graduate* — now what?

What makes a great ending? Give them what they expect and then something more. Give them what they expect and then surprise them one more time.

TO DO:

Add five more events to your next column ending with the *Last Great Decision.*

Write the final page of your treatment.

CHAPTER THIRTEEN

Writing the Screenplay

Congratulations. You have broken the story. Most of the heavy lifting has been done. All you have to do now is write the script. But, unlike before, now you have some things to guide you on the journey:

- A POSTER
- A CORKBOARD WITH FORTY INDEX CARDS/FORTY EVENTS
- AN EIGHT-PAGE SCRIPTMENT OF WHAT HAPPENS IN YOUR STORY

You know what to write. Now write it.

A MUSIC LESSON

I love to write to a certain piece of music. Pick something that reflects the mood of what you are trying to write. I don't care if it's country, pop, classical, hip-hop. You are going to listen to it so much it's going to become white noise. The rule is *you can only listen to this music when writing your script.* If it comes on in the car when you are driving, turn it off. You want to condition your brain to think — oh, I know that song. I should be writing.

TURNING THE SCRIPTMENT INTO THE SCRIPT

You're done. You know your story. You have seen the movie in your head. It goes from A to B to C with enough interesting twists and turns to keep it, well, interesting. Is the hero different than who she was at the beginning? Are you different than you were at the beginning?

I hope that's a yes for both. As Michael Dorsey says at the end of *Tootsie*, the hard part is over...

Now you're going to turn the *scriptment* into a *script*.

How do you do that?

My first rule is *keep reading scripts*. Print out a few of your favorites. Keep reading what is out there so you always are learning and relearning the form.

WHY DO SCREENPLAYS FAIL?

Screenplays fail when there is not enough character and story to fill 120 pages. Well, check that off your list. We got that covered.

Screenplays also fail because *they don't read like screenplays*. Keep reading screenplays and you will see that the ones that have sold — good or bad — have the same thing in common. When you were finished reading them, you probably felt as if you had seen the movie. That is what you are striving for.

That cinematic experience on the page.

Your screenplay *has to read like a screenplay*. No eight-page dialogue scenes. Look at scripts. Some scenes are long — three pages. Some are short — 1/8th of a page. It varies.

Comedies tend to have lots of *white* on the page. They are sparse.

Read the dialogue out loud. Make sure it's tight.

Make sure that the act breaks are pronounced.

Your first assignment on writing your script is to *type up the first fifteen pages* of a similar script that has been produced. Find it. Type it.

What?

What a waste of time!

It's really not. You are going to be building muscles here. As your fingers dance on that keyboard, you will start to feel when a scene is ending, when dialogue breaks naturally.

So this way when you are writing your script, you can think to yourself: Hey, this scene is taking a lot longer to write than that scene I typed up. When you are done, come back here and we'll start on your script...

IMPORT THE SCRIPTMENT INTO SCREENWRITING SOFTWARE

Import the scriptment into a professional screenwriting program. There are two industry standards: Final Draft and Movie Magic Screenwriter.

The important thing is *keep your place marks*. Write down in your script document **END OF ACT ONE. LABEL THE SEQUENCES.**

What we're striving for here is to give you road marks as you go on the journey. So when you write that first sequence and it ends on page twenty-four of your screenplay and it says on the page END OF SEQUENCE A — you will know, this was supposed to take, like, fifteen pages. You'll know you have overshot your destination.

BREAK INTO LOCATIONS

Great. You placed all of your markers. Let's go to step two, *break into locations*. You are going to go through your scriptment and identify the *scene* locations within your prose.

Is it interior — INT?

Exterior — EXT?

Where does it take place?

When? DAY, NIGHT, LATER, THE NEXT DAY, CONTINUOUS.

These are all choices.

When do you do CUT TO? I like to save it to break up the sequences. Also to break up days within the story.

Use CUT TOs to reinforce *transitions*. If you want a huge impact, use SMASH CUT TO. For example, Dorothy Boyd is on the airplane with her son in *Jerry Maguire* and says, regarding Jerry:

```
                 DOROTHY
       Whoever snagged him must be
       one classy lady.

                 SMASH CUT TO:

Avery screams in orgasmic pleasure.
```

Otherwise be sparing with CUT TOs.

THE DIALOGUE PASS

This does not mean you are going to write the dialogue of the scene now. It's impossible to do, since we have yet to determine who is driving the scene and who/what is generating the conflict. Simply go through the expanded document and look for where someone says anything in text. When you wrote the scriptment, dialogue was important to you and I want you to keep it for now.

So break it into dialogue format.

TRACK THE CHARACTER

Read through the document again. Does my fool change? Go on a journey? Do we have intimacy through failure?

THE SCENE PASS

Look at the very first scene in your movie. Identify the three C's. You are going to do this for every scene in the scriptment.

(1) CHARACTER: Who is driving the scene? Whose scene is this? Who wants what in the scene?

(2) CONFLICT: What is stopping the character from achieving that?

(3) CHANGE: What changes happen in the scene? Does the end of the scene lead to the next scene?

Remember, the protagonist does not have to drive every scene in the movie. In *Jerry Maguire*, Bob Sugar takes Jerry to lunch to fire Jerry. That is his goal in the scene. Jerry is not driving the scene. He is reacting. Conflict occurs as the two men argue in the public place. There is *change* at the end of the scene as Jerry walks out, fired but wanting all his clients. Notice how the end of a scene leads to the beginning of the next scene.

As you expand the scriptment you want to be able to sit down and just worry about the writing.

Go through your entire document and do the three c's for every scene!

THE WRITING BEGINS

Oh no! I have to write this thing. Yes, you do. And it's not going to be easy. But it's easier now than when you first started reading this book.

Now you know what to write.

So, how are you going to write it?

I handed in my first studio assignment and the executive read it and said: "Great! You're sixty percent there!"

Sixty percent. That's failing, isn't it? That's okay. Because you can fix it. You can make it better. And right now the most important part is writing that vomit draft. Getting it out.

Really bad first drafts are allowed and encouraged. You can't rewrite what you have not written.

Focus on the essential things that you need to accomplish in this scene to move the plot forward. What do we need to learn and whom do we need to meet?

INCLUDE ONLY WHAT IS ESSENTIAL TO THE PLOT

Nothing goes on the page that does not go on the screen. (But the converse is not true… much is on the screen that is not on the page).

Be careful of the dreaded *HDWK* — the *How Do We Know*. That is, don't tell us a character is a womanizer — show us.

Cut camera direction. Be stingy with dialogue directions. Don't act for the actor, don't direct for the director.

Write in a way that is natural for you.

Give everyone a name.

However long it takes to read is how long it should play on the screen.

SOME WORDS ABOUT DIALOGUE

Not a lot has been written about movie dialogue. It is tough. It takes time. One of my daughters observed that it tends to be sarcastic. I agree. Movie characters always tend to say the witty thing. Bad dialogue is easy to identify. It goes on too long. It is clunky. It is on the nose.

Movie dialogue is not merely people talking. Good dialogue *reveals* character. It tells about the people in the story. When in doubt, have the characters talking about the events in the story.

Beware of Harry the Explainer: Someone who comes on the screen and explains everything that is going on in his life in one long never-ending passage. For my money, Lehman, Goldman, Wilder and Diamond are the best. Tarantino is great but hard to emulate.

A CARD A DAY

I sold a script when I was temping and had a six-month-old baby at home. Of course there was no YouTube or tweets back then to preoccupy me. You have to learn to turn off everything in your life and try to do a *card a day* from your board. Everyday. It's about one hour or less. In forty days you have a script. Yes, work on weekends. Do it. Each day you miss, the harder it is to get back into it.

I like to do a lot of *left margin writing.* I sketch out the beats of the scene on the left margin like this:

- Bill walks in
- house is a mess
- steps on a toy
- SQUEAK
- noise from upstairs...
- tries the lights
- don't work
- B/Hello?
- BANG! A bullet rips through his head.

Once I know the beats, I go back and write the prose.

Also, I like *leaving food on the table.* After finishing the scenes for that day, I will sketch out some of the beats for the next day's work. So when I sit back down the next day, I read what I plan on working on and get to work. I have left the food on the table — the beats for the next day are waiting for me.

TRUST THE WORK YOU HAVE DONE

Don't go back and try to perfect the first act until you finish that first draft.

Finish it.

That is the key.

The scriptment work enables you to have a solid structure, some good character transformation.

The first draft is about getting the dialogue and characters down. Subsequent revisions are about polishing it up.

HOW DO I KNOW WHEN IT'S DONE?

After finishing something you think is great, give it to some-one you trust. Get their feedback. Listen. Don't defend the intention of what you were going to write. Ask specific ques-tions that you might have. Try to get someone who is going to give you notes that are *on the page.* You don't want to give someone your comedy set in India and get feedback that says, Can it be a romance in Kentucky? You are looking for notes to make what you have written better.

How to take notes is one of the most important lessons you can learn.

A friend once said: Writers who argue live in little houses. I think a lot has changed since then. You have to find your voice and defend the passion that you have put on the page. If you are lucky enough to sell it, remember: Listen. Think about what the exec has to say, and then decide if you agree or disagree. Lots of times you can listen to the notes, wait a few days, then tell them you tried it and it didn't work. They are looking to be part of the creative process. Don't be con-frontational. Be smart.

THE BUSINESS OF WRITING

"How do I get an agent?" is the question I am always asked.

I asked it when I was breaking in. Here's an advantage you have. It's called the Internet. People are a few keystrokes away. People are accessible. CAA or WME are not accessible. Here's a tip — they were not accessible when I was a client there. Friends who are at the big agencies tend to also have a *manager* who does the bulk of the work.

QUERY LETTERS

So, how would I get an agent today if I were starting out? I would target managers. *The Hollywood Creative Directory* publishes addresses for all reps, including managers. Read the trades and take note of who is selling material similar to yours. Send an email or a letter. You might not get a reply, but you might.

A manager will help you get an agent. If you do target agents, go for the smaller places. They're hungrier. Look for personal connections. Where did they go to school? Mention you developed the script at (insert school you attended here!). Don't pitch the whole script; sell the sizzle.

CONTESTS

There are a lot of screenwriting contests out there. The most famous is the Nicholl Fellowship. I also like screenplay competitions within film festivals. See who the judges are on the panel. Lots of times agents and managers will attend those festivals. Target the festivals close to you. Attend. Mingle. Hollywood is a networking place.

I KNOW A GUY WHO KNOWS A GUY WHO KNOWS A GUY

The guy who wrote and directed the movie *Waiting* was living in Florida. He met a small-time producer who said he wanted to produce his script. The producer turned out to be a moron but the assistant liked the script and said she went to school with someone who was on Project Greenlight. She sent the script to that guy, who sent it to a manager, who called the guy in Florida wanting to rep him.

A guy who knows a guy…

The Farrelly Brothers broke in when they gave their script to someone whose parents lived next door to Eddie Murphy. Well the girl, when visiting her parents, saw Eddie and gave him the script. Eddie, as a favor, read it and loved it. Problem was the Farrellys forget to put their name and contact info on the script. One night they were watching Letterman, who was interviewing Eddie Murphy, who tells the story of this great script he read but can't find the writers. The next day, Peter and Bobby were on the phone.

THE D-BOYS AND D-GIRLS

My wife and I moved to LA with a script in hand. We called everyone we knew. One person who had been kicked out of NYU film school was now working in development for a producer (she was a D-Girl). She agreed to read our script, liked it, and asked if we would do some work on it. Now, we could easily have said: Pay us and we'll do it. Then she would have said, "To the hell with you, I'm a professional." We sat down and listened to her thoughts and they were very helpful. (There are a hell of lot of smart people out here). We did the notes. She gave it to her boss who wanted to submit it to the studio. We agreed — but now was the time to *ask for something*. We said sure, but help get us an agent. The producer was glad to help and, with his recommendation, we landed our first agent. We were in the game.

We made our contact through a graduate school connection. That is what you have to do. Find the people in the business who have something in common with you. Then ask, be polite. All they can do is say no.

FUNNY IS MONEY

One of my favorite movies of all time is Preston Sturges's *Sullivan's Travels*. It's about a film director who has made musicals and comedies and now wants to make a serious film. You know, the kind they love at Oscar time. The film takes place during the Great Depression. Think: like the Great Recession but in black and white. Anyway the director comes full circle and realizes laughter is more important than he ever realized.

We started this fool's journey together, agreeing that there is not enough laughter in the world. It's up to you now. There is no better feeling in the world than making people laugh, laughing at work… and getting paid for it.

I love teaching comedy film writing because it reminds me of what I love to do in life. I have not yet had the success I have sought on the screen, but I have had it on the page. And in the classroom.

I hope someday to hear that someone has read my book and that it has inspired him or her to write a movie that made the world a little happier — at least for ninety minutes.

Sometimes that's all we need.

FILMOGRAPHY

10 (1979)

40-Year-Old Virgin, The (2005)

48 Hours (1982)

300 (2006)

500 Days of Summer (2009)

Abbott and Costello Go to Mars (1953)

Abbott and Costello Meet Frankenstein (1948)

Abbott and Costello Meet the Invisible Man (1951)

Abbott and Costello Meet the Killer (1949)

Ace Ventura: Pet Detective (1994)

Adam's Rib (1949)

Adventureland (2009)

Airplane! (1980)

All of Me (1984)

Almost Famous (2000)

American Graffiti (1973)

American Pie (1999)

American President, The (1995)

American Wedding (2003)

American Werewolf in London (1981)

Analyze This (1999)

Anchorman: The Legend of Ron Burgundy (2004)

Animal Crackers (1930)

Annie Hall (1977)

Apartment, The (1960)

Arthur (1981)

As Good As It Gets (1997)

Avatar (2009)

Baby Boom (1987)

Bachelor Party (1984)

Back to the Future (1985)

Bad Boys (1995)

Bad News Bears, The (1976)

Ball of Fire (1941)

Banger Sisters, The (2002)

Beach Blanket Bingo (1965)

Being There (1979)

Ben Hur (1959)

Best in Show (2000)

Beverly Hills Cop (1984)

Big (1988)

Big Chill, The (1983)

Big Green, The (1995)

Bill and Ted's Excellent Adventure (1989)

Billy Hollywood's Screen Test (1998)

Birdcage, The (1996)

Blazing Saddles (1974)

Blow-Up (1966)

Bob & Carol & Ted & Alice (1969)

Bondu Saved From Drowning (1932)

Borat: Cultural Learnings of America for Make Benefit Glorious Nation of Kazakhstan (2006)

Born Yesterday (1950)

Bottle Rocket (1996)

Boys Night Out (1962)

Boys on the Side (1995)

Breakfast at Tiffany's (1961)

Breakfast Club, The (1985)

Break-Up, The (2006)

Bridget Jones's Diary (2001)

Bringing Up Baby (1938)

Broadcast News (1987)

Brokeback Mountain (2005)

Bruce Almighty (2003)

Buck Privates (1941)

Bull Durham (1988

Bullets Over Broadway (1994)

Caddyshack (1980)

Cat Ballou (1965)

Catch-22 (1970)

CB4 (1993)

Chasing Amy (1997)

Chinatown (1974)

Cinderella Story, A (2004)

Cinderfella (1950)

Citizen Kane (1941)

Citizen Ruth (1996)

City Slickers (1991)

Date Night (2010)

Dave (1993)

Deerhunter, The (2009)

Diner (1982)

Dodgeball (2004)

Down and Out in Beverly Hills (1986)

Dr. Horrible's Sing-Along Blog (2008)

Dr. Strangelove or How I Learned to Stop Worrying and Love the Bomb (1964)

Duck Soup (1933)

Due Date (2010)

Dumb and Dumber (1994)

Ed Wood (1994)

Enchanted (2007)

Errand Boy, The (1961)

Eurotrip (2004)

*Everything You Wanted to Know About Sex *But Were Afraid to Ask* (1972)

Exorcist, The (1973)

Fast Times at Ridegmont High (1982)

Father of the Bride (1950)

Father of the Bride (1991)

Ferris Bueller's Day Off (1986)

Finding Nemo (2003)

Fish Called Wanda, A (1988)

Flirting With Disaster (1996)

Fools Rush In (1997)

Forgetting Sarah Marshall (2008)

Fortune Cookie, The (1966)

Foul Play (1978)

Four Christmases (2008)

Four Weddings and a Funeral (1994)

French Kiss (1995)

Freshman, The (1925)

Front Page, The (1931)

Front Page, The (1974)

Funny Thing Happened On the Way to the Forum, A (1966)

Galaxy Quest (1999)

General, The (1926)

Get Him to the Greek (2010)

Get Shorty (1995)

Ghost Breakers, The (1940)

Ghostbusters (1984)

Giant (1956)

Girl Next Door, The (2004)

Glass Bottom Boat, The (1966)

Godfather, The (1972)

Gold Rush, The (1925)

Goldfinger (1964)

Good Morning, Vietnam (1987)

Goodbye Girl, The (1977)

Graduate, The (1967)

Grease (1978)

Great McGinty, The (1940

Great Race, The (1965)

Groundhog Day (1993)

Grumpy Old Men (1993)

Guess Who? (2005)

Guess Who's Coming to Dinner (1967)

Hangover, The (2009)

Hannah and Her Sisters (1986)

Hard Day's Night, A (1964)

Harold and Kumar Go to White Castle (2004)

Harry Potter and the Sorcerer's Stone (2001)

Heartbreak Kid, The (1972)

Heartbreak Kid, The (2007)

Heaven Can Wait (1978)

Here Comes Mr. Jordan (1941)

His Girl Friday (1940)

Hitch (2005)

Holiday, The (2006)

Home Alone (1990)

Honeymoon in Vegas (1992)

Hot Shots! (1991)

House Boat (1958)

I Love You, Alice B. Tolkas (1968)

I Love You, Man (2009)

I Married A Witch (1942)

I Was a Male War Bride (1949)

I.Q. (1994)

In & Out (1997)

In-Laws, The (1979)

Ishtar (1987)

It Happened One Night (1934)

It's A Mad, Mad, Mad, Mad World (1963)

It's a Wonderful Life (1946)

It's Complicated (2009)

Jaws (1975)

Jerk, The (1979)

Jerry Maguire (1996)

Julie & Julia (2009)

Juno (2007)

Just Wright (2010)

Kid, The (1921)

Kingpin (1996)

Kiss Me, Guido (1997)

Kissing Jessica Stein (2001)

Knocked Up (2007)

La Cage aux Folles (1978)

La Totale (1991)

Lady Eve, The (1941)

Ladykillers, The (1955)

Lars and The Real Girl (2007)

Lavender Hill Mob, The (1951)

League of Their Own, A (1992)

Legally Blonde (2001)

Liar, Liar (1997)

Little Miss Sunshine (2006)

Longest Yard, The (1974)

Lord of the Rings: Fellowship of the Ring (2001)

Lottery Ticket (2010)

Love at First Bite (1979)

Lover Come Back (1961)

M.A.S.H. (19700

Major and The Minor, The (1942)

Major League (1989)

Man on the Moon (1999)

Manhattan (1979)

Married to the Mob (1988)

Mask, The (1994)

Meet The Parents (2000)

Melinda and Melinda (2004)

Men in Black (1997)

Michael (1996)

Midnight (1939)

Midnight Run (1988)

Mighty Aphrodite (1995)

Mighty Ducks (1992)

Miracle on 34th Street (1947)

Miss Congeniality (2000)

Monkey Business (1952)

Monty Python and the Holy Grail (1975)

Moonstruck (1987)

Mr. and Mrs. Smith (2005)

My Best Friend's Wedding (1997)

My Big Fat Greek Wedding (2002)

My Favorite Blonde (1942)

My Favorite Brunette (1947)

My Favorite Year (1982)

National Lampoon's Animal House (1978)

National Lampoon's European Vacation (1985)

National Lampoon's Vacation (1983)

Network (1976)

New Leaf, A (1971)

Night at the Museum (2006)

Ninotchka (1939)

North by Northwest (1959)

Notting Hill (1999)

Nutty Professor, The (1963)

Nutty Professor, The (1996)

Oceans 11 (2001)

Odd Couple, The (1968)

Office Space (1999)

Oh, God! (1977)

Old School (2003)

Operation Petticoat (1959)

Outrageous Fortune (1987)

Parenthood (1989)

Pat and Mike (1952)

Philadelphia Story, The (1940)

Pillow Talk (1959)

Pineapple Express (2008)

Planes, Trains and Automobiles (1987)

Pretty in Pink (1986)

Pretty Woman (1990)

Private Benjamin (1980)

Private Parts (1997)

Prizzi's Honor (1985)

Producers, The (1968)

Producers, The (2005)

Proposal, The (2009)

Prudence and the Pill (1968)

Purple Rose of Cairo, The (1985)

Raiders of the Lost Ark (1981)

Reefer Madness (1936)

Revenge of the Nerds (1984)

Risky Business (1983)

Road to Morocco (1942)

Road to Rio (1947)

Road to Utopia (1946)

Rocky (1976)

Roman Holiday (1953)

Romy and Michele's High School Reunion (1997)

Runaway Bride (1999)

Scarface (1983)

Scary Movie (2000)

School of Rock (2003)

Scream (1996)

Sex Drive (2008)

Sex in the City (2008)

Shakespeare in Love (1998)

Shampoo (1975)

Shane (1953)

Shaun of the Dead (2004)

She's Gotta Have It (1986)

She's the Man (2006)

Sherlock Jr. (1924)

Shot in the Dark, A (1964)

Shrek (2001)

Silence of the Lambs, The (1991)

Singin' in the Rain (1952)

Sixteen Candles (1984)

Slapshot (1977)

Sleeper (1973)

Sleepless in Seattle (1993)

Small Time Crooks (2000)

Smokey and the Bandit (1977)

Some Like It Hot (1959)

Something's Gotta Give (2003)

Sophie's Choice (1982)

Speed (1994)

Splash (1984)

Starting Over (1979)

Stripes (1981)

Sullivan's Travels (1941)

Superbad (2007)

Sure Thing, The (1985)

Surrogates, The (2009)

Sweet Home Alabama (2002)

Sweetest Thing, The (2002)

Swingers (1996)

Take the Money and Run (1969)

Teen Wolf (1985)

Ten Commandments, The (1956)

Terminator 2 (1991)

Terminator, The (1984)

Terms of Endearment (1983)

Thank You For Smoking (2005)

That Touch of Mink (1962)

The Big Lebowski (1998

There's a Girl In My Soup (1970)

There's Something About Mary (1998)

This is Spinal Tap (1984)

Tin Cup (1996)

To Die For (1995)

Tootsie (1982)

Tortilla Soup (2001)

Trading Places (1983)

Tropic Thunder (2008)

True Lies (1994)

Unforgiven, The (1992)

Untouchables, The (1987)

Up in Smoke (1978)

Up in the Air (2009)

Wag the Dog (1997)

Waiting (2005)

War of the Roses, The (1989)

Wayne's World (1992)

We're No Angels (1955)

We're No Angels (1989)

Wedding Banquet, The (1993)

Wedding Crashers (2005)

Wedding Singer, The (1998)

West Side Story (1961)

What About Bob? (1991)

What Happens in Vegas (2008)

What Woman Want (2000)

When Harry Met Sally (1989)

Where the Boys Are (1960)

While You Were Sleeping (1995)

White Men Can't Jump (1992)

Who's Afraid of Virginia Woolf? (1966)

Whole Nine Yards, The (2000)

Witches of Eastwick, The (1987)

Witness (1985)

Wizard of Oz, The (1939)

Working Girl (1988)

You Don't Mess With the Zohan (2008)

You've Got Mail (1998)

Young Frankenstein (1974)

Zack and Miri Make a Porno (2008)

Zero Hour (1957)

ABOUT THE AUTHOR

Keith Giglio has been hired and fired by most studios in his eighteen years as a screenwriter in Los Angeles. He has received credit on seven-and-a-half movies and has written and sold over twenty screenplays.

As co-screenwriter/producer he has worked on *A Cinderella Story* and served as Story Consultant on *Disney's Tarzan*. Other credits include *Noah, Joshua, Return to Halloweentown,* and subsequent *A Cinderella Story* sequels.

His first WGA job writing gigs were adapting *Archie* into a screenplay for Universal and working on the *Vacation* franchise for Warner Brothers. He has co-written scripts for Bruce Willis, Bette Midler, and other famous people whose first name begins with B.

His unproduced screenplay *Beer Boy* was cited by the WGA as one of the best unproduced comedies. If it ever gets produced, he will be glad to return the honor.

He has enjoyed many years of writing with his wife, Juliet, until she got tired of his jokes and discovered sane people do not spend their days in a room with Keith. Unfortunately, his students are a captive audience.

Keith has taught screenwriting at the Writers Program at UCLA Extension, where was he named Instructor of the Year in 2009. Keith is a screenwriting professor at Syracuse University's renowned Newhouse School. Keith can be reached at keith@inappropriategoal.com but will only hear an elevator pitch in an elevator.

You can follow the comedic exploits of Keith on Twitter at @keithgiglio or on his website, www.inappropriategoal.com.

YOU'RE FUNNY!
TURN YOUR SENSE OF HUMOR
INTO A LUCRATIVE NEW CAREER

D.B. GILLES

You're Funny! is the next best thing to being in a comedy writing class. It covers the different ways to earn a living as a comedy writer, including writing sitcoms, jokes for late night talk shows, parody, stand up, and screenwriting and will help you determine if you can actually make a living writing jokes and making people laugh.

"Fast. Funny. Informative. D.B. Gilles has written a delightful book about tapping into your inner funny. Read it. You'll laugh. You'll learn."

> — Matt Williams, co-creator/producer, *Roseanne,*
> *Home Improvement*; director, *Where The Heart Is*

"D.B. is a positive force for comedy. This book is a funny, entertaining, and practical guide for anyone wanting to break into the world of comedy writing."

> — Jeff Cox, writer, *Blades of Glory*

"You're Funny! is one of the best books available on comedy writing with a 24 carat gold payoff-specific guidance on how to turn those skills into a profitable career."

> — Don DeMaio, teacher, American Comedy Institute, NYC

"You're Funny! is the first how-to handbook that ever got me laughing out loud. A long-time student of the comedy game, D.B. knows his stuff and is damned funny in passing the secrets on. A real treat."

> — David McKenna, co-author of *Memo From The Story Department*

D.B. GILLES has taught comedy writing and screenwriting in the Undergraduate Film & Television Department at New York University's Tisch School of the Arts for nearly 20 years. He is the author of *The Screenwriter Within: How to Turn The Movie in Your Head Into a Salable Screenplay* and *The Portable Film School.* He is co-author of the George Bush parody *W. The First Hundred Days: A White House Journal.* D.B. is also a script consultant and writing coach. He writes the popular blog *Screenwriters Rehab: For Screenwriters Who Can't Get Their Acts Together.* His new play *Sparkling Object* opened last year in New York.

$19.95 · 185 PAGES · ORDER NUMBER 160RLS · ISBN: 9781932907957

THE SCRIPT-SELLNG GAME - 2ND ED.
A HOLLYWOOD INSIDER'S LOOK AT GETTING YOUR SCRIPT SOLD AND PRODUCED

KATHIE FONG YONEDA

The Script-Selling Game is about what they never taught you in film school. This is a look at screenwriting from the other side of the desk — from a buyer who wants to give writers the guidance and advice that will help them to not only elevate their craft but to also provide them with the down-in-the-trenches information of what is expected of them in the script selling marketplace.

It's like having a mentor in the business who answers your questions and provides you with not only valuable information, but real-life examples on how to maneuver your way through the Hollywood labyrinth. While the first edition focused mostly on film and television movies, the second edition includes a new chapter on animation and another on utilizing the Internet to market yourself and find new opportunities, plus an expansive section on submitting for television and cable.

"I've been writing screenplays for over 20 years. I thought I knew it all — until I read The Script-Selling Game. *The information in Kathie Fong Yoneda's fluid and fun book really enlightened me. It's an invaluable resource for any serious screenwriter."*

> — Michael Ajakwe Jr., Emmy-winning TV producer, *Talk Soup*; Executive Director of Los Angeles Web Series Festival (LAWEBFEST); and creator/ writer/director of *Who...* and *Africabby* (AjakweTV.com)

"Kathie Fong Yoneda knows the business of show from every angle and she generously shares her truly comprehensive knowledge — her chapter on the Web and new media is what people need to know! She speaks with the authority of one who's been there, done that, and gone on to put it all down on paper. A true insider's view."

> — Ellen Sandler, former co-executive producer of *Everybody Loves Raymond* and author of *The TV Writer's Workbook*

KATHIE FONG YONEDA has worked in film and television for more than 30 years. She has held executive positions at Disney, Touchstone, Disney TV Animation, Paramount Pictures Television, and Island Pictures, specializing in development and story analysis of both live-action and animation projects. Kathie is an internationally known seminar leader on screenwriting and development and has conducted workshops in France, Germany, Austria, Spain, Ireland, Great Britain, Australia, Indonesia, Thailand, Singapore, and throughout the U.S. and Canada.

$19.95 · 248 PAGES · ORDER NUMBER 161RLS · ISBN 13: 9781932907919

{ THE MYTH OF MWP }

In a dark time, a light bringer came along, leading the curious and the frustrated to clarity and empowerment. It took the well-guarded secrets out of the hands of the few and made them available to all. It spread a spirit of openness and creative freedom, and built a storehouse of knowledge dedicated to the betterment of the arts.

The essence of the Michael Wiese Productions (MWP) is empowering people who have the burning desire to express themselves creatively. We help them realize their dreams by putting the tools in their hands. We demystify the sometimes secretive worlds of screenwriting, directing, acting, producing, film financing, and other media crafts.

By doing so, we hope to bring forth a realization of 'conscious media' which we define as being positively charged, emphasizing hope and affirming positive values like trust, cooperation, self-empowerment, freedom, and love. Grounded in the deep roots of myth, it aims to be healing both for those who make the art and those who encounter it. It hopes to be transformative for people, opening doors to new possibilities and pulling back veils to reveal hidden worlds.

MWP has built a storehouse of knowledge unequaled in the world, for no other publisher has so many titles on the media arts. Please visit www.mwp.com where you will find many free resources and a 25% discount on our books. Sign up and become part of the wider creative community!

Onward and upward,

Michael Wiese
Publisher/Filmmaker